Susan Bradford

Royal Blood Lies

The Inside Story on How the Rothschilds Took Over the British Monarchy, Purged Royals, Created Puppet Leaders, Waged Revolutions, Corrupted Morals and Institutions, Plundered Wealth, Created False Realities, and Pitted Nations, Societies, and Peoples Against Each Other in a Ruthless, Megalomaniacal Quest for World Domination

By Susan Bradford

And did those feet in ancient time
Walk upon England's mountains green
And was the Holy Lamb of God
On England's pleasant pastures seen
And did the countenance divine
Shine forth upon our clouded hills
And was Jerusalem built here
Among those dark Satanic mills
Bring me my bow of burning gold!
Bring me my arrows of desire!
Bring me my spear o'clouds unfold!
Bring me my chariots of fire
I will not cease from mental fight;
Nor shall my sword sleep in my hand
Till we have built Jerusalem
In England's green and pleasant land

Vangelis

Table of Contents

Other Books by This Author

UNMASKED: THE CORONAVIRUS STORY
The Nauseating Truth Behind the Global Quest to Bring the World to Heel, Destroy Nationalism, and Undermine the Trump Presidency through Fake Scandals, Simulated Pandemics, Junk Science, Political Puppets, Brazen Extortion, and Rapacious Money Grabs

FLEECED:
Elon Musk, The Green New Deal, and the Coming Technocracy as Revealed through the Oklahoma Indian Land Scam

THE FULL COURT PRESS:
How the Bush Administration Managed the Media through Embedded Reporters, Talking Points, Black Lists, Intimidation, Back Channels, and Clever PR
(Foreword by Senior CBS Foreign Correspondent Tom Fenton)

LYNCHED!
The Shocking Story of How the Political Establishment Manufactured a Scandal to Have Republican Superlobbyist Jack Abramoff Removed from Power

THE TRIBES THAT ROCKEFELLER BUILT:
The Inside Story of How Big Oil and Industry Are Working with and through the Federal Government and Indian Tribes to Shore up Markets

UNITED CHURCH OF HEIST:
How Barack Obama and the Ecumenicists Transformed the United Church of Christ into a Political Machine for the Democratic Party

THE SHADOW DRAGON:
The Inside Story Behind Donald Trump's Struggle to Derail the Deep State

THE SECOND AMERICAN REVOLUTION:
How the Bolsheviks Waged and Lost the Second American Revolution

About the Author

Susan Bradford is a writer, author, and a public speaker who provides commentary and analysis on foreign policy, realpolitik, and the machinations of the Deep State. Her books are dedicated to pulling back the curtain on corruption within governmental and financial institutions for the purposes of transparency, accountability, and genuine reform. Susan has written and ghost written many books and articles and appeared on the BBC, podcasts, radio programs, and most recently, a documentary on the Great Reset.

As an undergraduate at U.C. Irvine, Susan earned a BA in English and spent her junior year abroad at the University of St. Andrews in Scotland. She earned her Master's degree in International Relations from the University of Essex where she worked as Senior Research Fellow for the Atlantic Council of the UK and as Essex representative on the NATO Universities Advisory Committee. During her postgraduate matriculation, she founded *The European Review*, which became the departmental publication for the Centre for European Studies at Essex. As Editor, she solicited and edited manuscripts from heads of state on European integration, interviewed Baron Robert Rothschild and other elites on globalism, and covered such historic events as the Council of Europe Summit in Madrid which launched the euro; the Britain in the World conference in London; and an anti-NATO debate in the Russian state Duma. She was also acting editor of the *New Atlantic Initiatives*, the newsletter for the eponymous declaration which called for the creation of a TAFTA.

Susan has worn many hats in the field of communications and has worked, for example, as news writer for KNX (CBS) news radio, reporter for City News Service, production assistant for the PBS Red Car Film Project, producer for Fox News Channel, assignments editor for the Voice of America, speech writer for Korean Ambassador Sung Chul Yang, and speech writer UK Shadow Foreign Secretary Michael Howard.

Susan covered the O.J. Simpson murders and was lead investigative journalist on the Abramoff investigation, the nation's most far reaching federal corruption probe in which she exposed the machinations behind this partisan prosecution of superlobbyist Jack Abramoff. She has been breaking news ever since.

Susan's website is: **www.susanbradford.org**.

Author's Remarks

I began my research on *Royal Blood Lies* tracing the bloodlines surrounding the House of Windsor. I knew that the Rothschild banking family had financed both sides of the American Revolution and all sides of the Napoleonic Wars. Through the Napoleonic Wars, the Rothschild dynasty acquired financial control of France; crashed the British stock market to acquire breeding rights into the British Royal family; placed the Vatican in its debt; and dissolved the Holy Roman Empire.

Like many Americans, I knew little about the Holy Roman Empire, and so I dug a little deeper. Soon I found myself transfixed by the Roman Empire, its antecedent. I was reminded of Edward Gibbon's *The History of the Decline and Fall of the Roman Empire,* which I had read in high school for my Honors Western Civilization class. My wonderful teacher, Adrianne Phillips, who instilled in me a lifelong love of history, instructed her students to study Gibbon's books for insight on how empires rise and fall while drawing parallels with the United States. There were many parallels then and ominously, far more now. Little did I know, the origins of the cabal that now confounds humanity had its origins in ancient Rome.

I knew that Sir Francis Bacon and Sir Walter Raleigh, the swashbuckling defenders of the faith, had written together under the pen name of William Shakespeare and encoded the secrets of elites within the works of the famous bard. As I reread Shakespeare, I noticed that Bacon and Raleigh were directing the audience's attention back to Rome and to Venice while working with the East India Company to establish colonies and markets in the Americas. Suddenly I was exploring all sorts of fascinating connections that served as the inspiration for this book. They all trace back to the "divine right to rule," which was established in Rome.

Once this right had been usurped, Western Civilization was placed on a dangerous trajectory toward global tyranny. This book is intended to open eyes to avert this catastrophic fate for humanity.

I.
Nation Under God

French Enlightened philosopher François-Marie Arouet, who was known by his nom de plume 'Voltaire,' once revealed, "Mais Henri s'avancait a sa grandeur supreme par des chemins caches inconnus a lui-meme." ("But Henry was advancing to his supreme grandeur by hidden paths unknown to himself.") A hidden hand guided history, though few were actually aware of its influence. Some attributed that force to God or to destiny, but what if the architect of civilization were simply an individual or a group of people executing God's will?

A 17th century adventurous duo known as Sir Walter Raleigh and Sir Francis Bacon knew the source of the hidden hand to be the Monarch, who was serving as God's representative on earth. Through freemasons and other secret societies, the Monarch's divine will was executed. In order to rule, the King or Queen was required to be initiated into the Egyptian mystery schools, the Christian faith, and to have descended from a sacred bloodline that traced to ancient Rome.

While European powers were establishing colonies around the world, Queen Elizabeth I, who held the divine right to rule, sent Raleigh and Bacon on a divine journey to explore the North American continent to explore territory and establish markets for the Crown "by the grace of God."

Raleigh accepted the challenge and chartered the path for the Pilgrims who arrived at Plymouth Rock in 1620. He also launched an expedition to Roanoke Island, establishing Virginia, named after his beloved Virgin Queen. Bacon, whom the future President Thomas Jefferson eulogized as "one of the greatest men (who) ever lived, without exception," recorded his adventures with Raleigh in a partially completed book, *New Atlantis*.

The historically accurate novel depicted the American colonies as an imaginary land called Bensalem. Upon reaching the shores, the characters were asked: "Are ye Christians?"

The weary travelers affirmed that they were, "fearing the less, because of the cross we had seen in the subscription (as) the person lifted up his right hand towards Heaven."

"If ye will swear by the merits of the Savior, that ye are no pirates, nor have shed blood, lawfully, nor unlawfully within forty days past, you may have license to come on land," they were told.

Before the Pilgrims could enter this blessed land, the travelers were required to take an oath pledging their fealty to God.

"We were all ready to take that oath." they said.

Thanks to the enterprise and ingenuity of Raleigh and Bacon, the colonies were founded. Yet, all was not quiet or peaceful as lurking in the shadows were the Venetian pirates who were all too ready to spill blood and betray the faith if private gain was to be had.

As members of the Elizabethan court, Raleigh and Bacon were privy to old world treachery and court intrigue, having interacted with the merchants of Venice and powerful Venetian oligarchs through the East India Company. By this point, the Venetian Empire was in decline while Great Britain was rising as a maritime power. After the Venetian Empire crumbled under the weight of its own corruption, the merchants of Venice scoped the horizons for new opportunities. To this end, they engaged the Merchants of London to establish new trading routes that the Venetians planned to commandeer for themselves. Slowly and steadily they planned to dominate the seas again and rule the commercial world, with their agents firmly implanted within the British Monarchy.

The Venetians mocked the quaint values of the British who believed in the "divine right to rule." Why serve God when it was so much more fun to serve oneself, without being restrained by conscience, empathy, or humanitarian principles? If they had to pretend to be Christians or Jews to get in with the Merchants of London and the earnest colonists, so be it. The ruthless Venetians would be running the show soon enough. Today, the colonies, tomorrow the world.

All actions undertaken by the Venetians were based upon

rational self-interest, with good faith given just enough expression to lower a rival's guard so that an advantage could be had. Concessions were born out of weakness. Why share bounty, when it could be horded for oneself? The people were not be protected or nurtured, but browbeaten, exploited, stripped of their assets, and reduced to slaves. They were true psychopaths who charmed with their tales of piracy and derring-do set in a backdrop of chests overflowing with exotic treasures acquired through global plunder.

Bacon and Raleigh smiled knowingly as they engaged the merchants. The discerning men were quickly onto the con; they not only wrote about the predatory activities under the pen name of Shakespeare but had actors dramatize Venetian skulduggery as if to hold up a mirror. One Shakespearean play, *Hamlet,* was first performed on the *Red Dragon*, an East India Company ship anchored off the coast of Sierra Leone. Another ship bore the name *The Scourge of Malice* to celebrate treacherous Venetian strategies. In *The Merchant of Venice,* Shakespeare eviscerated the Venetian merchants thoroughly while encouraging the Venetians to repent and convert to Christianity.

In *Merchants*, a banker extends a loan to a merchant on the condition that if the borrower were to default on the loan, he would have to give the lender a pound of his own flesh, hinting that the banker might potentially be a murderer, cannibal, or practitioner of black arts. Predictably, the lender defaults on the loan and is ordered to repay the banker with a pound of his own flesh. In desperation, the lender takes his case before the Venetian Court of Justice where the judge convicts the banker of attempted murder and orders him to give half of his wealth to merchant and the other half to Venice. As a good Christian, the merchant is merciful toward the banker who agrees to convert to Christianity to have his sentence reduced.

With the cabal's obsession with rewriting history and whitewashing its own treachery, *The Merchant of Venice* has been removed from libraries and book stores over concerns that it somehow perpetuates Jewish stereotypes. However the stereotypes perpetuated are not Jewish, but Venetian. Moreover, neither Bacon nor Raleigh were antisemitic. Rather, they were taking aim at the Venetians who hijacked the Jewish religion and assumed Jewish identifies in order to claim Jerusalem for the Antichrist and acquire personal gain under the banner of Judaism.

Jewish merchants had worked with Bacon and Raleigh to establish companies in the colonies. They also established commercial code based upon Judaic law. Jews had even accompanied William the Conqueror on his march through Great Britain and served as faithful advisors and allies with Christian Monarchs and Christian people. Raleigh had himself lived among Huguenots, French Protestants who challenged antisemitic Catholics. French Huguenots would later provide safe haven to persecuted Jews in Vichy (Nazi) France as documented in Philip Hallie's *Lest Innocent Blood be Shed.* While donning the identity of Christians and Jews – or whatever religion might best suit their purposes or advance their goals for plunder and world domination, the warrior-merchants of Venice persecuted Jews, Muslims, and Christians in equal measure.

Praising Jewish contributions to the new world while differentiating the Jewish merchants in the colonies from the fake Jewish merchants of Venice who had infiltrated their ranks, Bacon wrote: "A merchant of that city, whose name was Joabin … was a Jew and circumcised: for they have some few Jews yet remaining among them, whom they leave to their own religion. Which they may the better do, because they are of a far differing disposition from the Jews in other parts. For whereas they hate the name of Christ; and have a secret inbred rancor against the people among whom they live: these give unto our Savior many high attributes, and love the nation of Bensalem extremely."

Corporate Raiders

In the 17th century, the Venetian empire was in decline, and its merchants were getting desperate. Competition for trade was fierce. In the interests of establishing new markets for the British

Empire, the Merchants of London reached out to the Queen for assistance. In 1600, Queen Elizabeth I chartered the East India Company "by the grace of God" so that the Merchants of London could increase the realm's trade in the East Indies, Africa, and Asia for the "honor of our nation" and the "wealth of our people." At the same time, the Monarchy sought to break the Dutch monopoly in the spice trade.

As agents of the Crown, Sir Walter Raleigh and Sir Francis Bacon were actively involved in launching the East India Company. "We sailed from Peru for China and Japan, by the South Sea," Bacon wrote in *The New Atlantis*. "Now for our traveling from henna into parts abroad, our Lawgiver thought fit altogether to restrain it.... The Chinese sail where they will or can; which sheweth that their law of keeping out strangers is a law of pusillanimity and fear. But this restraint of ours hath one only exception, which is admirable; preserving the good which cometh by communicating with strangers, and avoiding the hurt.... But thus you see we maintain a trade not for gold, silver, or jewels; nor for silks; nor for spices; nor any other commodity of matter; but only for God's first creature, which was light: to have light of the growth of all parts of the world."

As the the Venetians slowly infiltrated its ranks, the India Company transformed into a vehicle for piracy, slavery, and imperialism. In one play, *Othello,* Shakespeare depicts a Venetian general who murders his own wife after a jealous rival tricks him. Corruption and wickedness were rampant throughout the East India Company.

After the East India Company transformed into a joint stock company, its merchants began trafficking in slaves, even though the colonies and Great Britain rejected slavery as an offense against God. Since Christians had been slaves during the Roman Empire, and Jews had been enslaved in Egypt, neither wanted to bring slavery to the colonies. In contrast, gunboat diplomacy provided Venetians a steady supply of slaves from which they could profit through human trafficking. After the plague killed a substantial portion of the European workforce, slave trading became an extremely lucrative business.

By the 1630s, the EIC had abandoned its operations in the East Indies to concentrate on its trade in Indian textiles and Chinese tea. The pirates of the East India Company set up local governments to administer the new territories they had conquered while locals were enslaved, exterminated, imprisoned in concentration camps, and otherwise exploited. Local armies accompanied the merchants to guard the ill gotten loot, quell uprisings, and reinforce the power and status of the imperialists, creating an unstoppable force.

Opium: The Drug of Priests

By the 18th century, the British East India Company was intervening in Indian, Chinese, and North American political affairs. The company had even acquired its own military to advance a new type of gunboat diplomacy and mercantilism that wiped out the rival French East India Company in 1752 and eliminated the Dutch East India Company in 1759.

By 1813, public outrage compelled the East India Company to abandon its detestable human trafficking operation. It then went on to expand its empire into India, a Rothschild venture that would devastate that continent. Since the Venetians were less interested in enhancing British maritime dominance than they were in claiming the world's wealth and power for themselves, the merchants eventually set out to dismantle the British Empire piece-by-piece. Once the colonies were separated from Mother England, the shadow Venetians claimed those territories for themselves and then set up representative governments "for the people," with the merchants, bankers, and mercenary armies secretly controlling them.

While working with the East India Company, the Venetians discovered that priests used opium for rituals that helped them "forget evil." Ancient Egyptians mixed opium with wine, spices, and water to form sedatives and aphrodisiacs that calmed crying babies, treated breast infections, reduced pain during surgical procedures, and inspired pleasure. In *Odyssey,* Homer depicts a drink called nepenthe, a veiled reference to opium, which Zeus' daughter, Helen, mixed with wine to assuage her painful memories. Warriors used opium to reduce the physical pain of injuries and heal their hearts after losing comrades in battles. Because of its addictive qualities, the drug was traditionally not used for recreational purposes but held in reserve for those who could use it responsibly.

The Venetians took something good and transformed it into something evil. As far as the Venetians were concerned, opium was the perfect drug to help lull people into passive compliance. More maliciously, the Venetians exploited the drug's addictive properties to line their own pockets through the public's indiscriminate use of the drug which they promoted, helping to establish international drug trafficking rings that would later work hand-in-hand with the the governments they controlled. "Welcome be a religion that pours into the bitter chalice of the suffering human species some sweet, soporific drops of spiritual opium, some drops of love, hope and faith," German writer Heinrich Hein wrote. At the time, the Bundestag reported that Germans in the Frankfurt ghettos were "attacking the Christian religion in the most impudent way, degrading existing conditions, and destroying all discipline and morality with belletristic writings accessible to all classes of readers." While the shadow imperial forces were attacking the religious, the religious were drowning their proverbial sorrows in opium.

The Rothschilds would later proclaim that "morality is for the masses." In a similar vein, a communist agitator, Karl Marx, whom the banking dynasty bankrolled to destabilize Europe in the 19th century, remarked that religion is the "opium of the masses," reflecting efforts by the Venetian bankers to co-opt that which the religious used for good into a force for evil. Soon the East India Company was trafficking in opium.

Devils at the Gate

The East India Company quickly ran up debts through its wars for empire, forcing the British Parliament, which controlled the public purse and oversaw colonial finances, to foot the bill. In response, Parliament passed the Tea Act of 1773, effectively putting colonial tea companies at a competitive disadvantage against the East India Company. In the scheme of things, tea was just one commodity and hardly an issue to get overly excited about. However, the Venetians seized upon the tea issue to establish a grievance to mobilize the people against the Monarchy; once the people were sufficiently outraged by the tax, colonists dressed as Indians dumped the tea in the Boston Harbor while proclaiming "no taxation without representation."

In truth, there was no reason for the people to act out in such a dramatic fashion as they enjoyed amicable relations with the Crown, and there were available diplomatic channels for them to negotiate taxes assessed on goods. The truth was, the Venetians were trying to stir up trouble in the colonies as part of a strategy to separate the colonies from the British Empire. Just like clockwork, the Boston Tea Party was followed by demands for revolution over unfair taxes on tea.

In the days that followed, tensions between the colonists and Great Britain flared up as agents of the Crown attempted to curtail Westward expansion on the North American continent. At the same time, Venetian merchants and their agents angled to seize land and natural resources for themselves. While the Indians and colonies were on friendly terms, Venetian agents armed Indians and directed them to attack the colonists to keep them off "their" land while arming colonial agitators to attack Indians and British agents. The Rothschilds provided the financing for these skirmishes and bankrolled the German Hessian mercenaries who were brought to North America to fight the colonists on behalf of the Crown. At the same time, Thomas Jefferson and other revolutionary leaders were on the Rothschild payroll to take up arms against Mother England.

While the Venetian merchants were working with the joint stock companies to forge new lines of business and lobbying the Crown to impose taxes on colonial goods, they were prompting the colonists to rebel. Once fighting broke out, the Venetians supplied 3,000 military personnel in the British royal navy to fight the colonists.

The Crown would not have any reason to curtain colonial expansion into the North American continent and would have had every reason to support the colonists as new land claimed would have fortified the Crown's tax base and territorial claims within North America. However, the Venetian merchants, who were serving the interests of Venetian oligarchs, were interested in cornering markets, eliminating competition, and claiming all the land, natural resources, and wealth in North America for themselves. In order for them to stake that claim, they would need to drive a wedge between the British Monarchy and its colonies, pit each side against each other and then place them in debt to bankers (like the Rothschilds). Once revolution had run its course, they would install a new "representative" government that stoked revolution premised on restoring power to the people.

The Republic that would emerge was to be based upon Plato's *Republic* in which the landowners and wealthy controlled the government while the poor and ordinary citizens had no stake

Once skirmishes broke out, blood flowed between both sides even though war had not been officially declared nor was it even desired by either side. The Monarchy was cognizant of the treasonous activities within the colonies. In a speech delivered before Parliament in October of 1775, King George III characterized the recurring rebellions as "traitorous" and expressed regret over the "effusion of the blood of my subjects....The unhappy may still retain their loyalty (to England) and may be too wise to see the fatal consequence of this usurpation, and wish to resist it, yet the torrent of violence has been strong enough to compel their acquiescence, till a sufficient force shall appear to support them."

What the colonists were experiencing was a Venetian-style coup that was engineered by corrupt shadowy interests to extinguish freedom on the North American continent and claim the wealth, labor, and resources in the new land for themselves. Had the colonists not been so law abiding and dedicated to public and private virtue, the skirmishes would have been far more violent and the consequences more dire. Once the colonists understood that England wanted peace, the Continent Congress extended an Olive Branch Petition to the King.

Efforts at reconciliation were sabotaged by revolutionaries guided and funded by shadowy foreign powers. Prior to the American Revolution, for example, Benjamin Franklin, an accomplished inventor and writer, was appointed Ambassador to England to represent all 13 colonies. Reflecting the influence of Venetian occultists, 1,200 human bones from over a dozen bodies, six of which belonged to children, were found buried in the basement of his house at 36 Craven Street, London, where Franklin lived as Ambassador to the Court of St. James. Forensics examiners determined that the victims died and were buried there during Franklin's ambassadorship.

In his capacity as Ambassador, Franklin recruited revolutionaries to stir up trouble in the colonies. For example, he processed the paperwork for Thomas Paine, an Englishman from Norfolk, to immigrate to North America. Once he arrived in the colonies, Paine wrote two seminal works, *Common Sense* and *The American Crisis*, which spelled out the arguments (propaganda) for the colonists to rebel against King George I.

Yet, Paine's sentiments were heavily steeped in ideology. They did not focus on specific grievances the colonies might have against King George I, but drew upon vague ideas from Enlightened thinkers invented and promulgated by shadow Venetian rulers as part of a wider strategy to acquire and expand their empires through perpetual revolution and war, while at the same time appealing to the public's sense of fairness and justice.

The idea was to seize upon a grievance around which the people would rally, portray the King as somehow responsible for the grievance, condemn the King as illegitimate, foment revolution against the so-called illegitimate King under the pretext of promoting fairness, liberty, and equality, topple the King, and then establish a new "representative government."

Since ideas were continually evolving, what was fair, ethical, and legal one day could be portrayed as unfair, unjust, and illegal the next. Therefore, revolution was a reliable and often used strategy for consolidating power. Shadow elites would subtly reshape and realign ideas and values without the public's direct knowledge or consent. Dissatisfaction could then be manufactured, resulting in demands for change that would inevitably serve to benefit the Venetians who professed to have the public's best interests at heart. As materialists, the solutions they promoted typically involved taking power and money away from one privileged group and giving it to another, with the spoils of revolution being given to themselves.

Paine's pamphlets were used as propaganda to stir up revolutionary fervor among the colonists. Amazingly, even though most colonists were opposed to war with Britain, the pamphlet sold 2.5 million copies, making it an instant best seller. Delighted with his newfound success, Paine approached the publisher to collect his profits only to discover that there weren't any to be had as the publication and distribution of his pamphlets had been privately subsidized, with few colonists actually buying or reading it. "The disposition of the people (was) such that they might have been led by a thread and government by a reed," Paine wrote, acknowledging the ease with which public opinion could be influenced to support the revolutionary cause.

At the same time, he acknowledged that the colonists were not eager for revolution. "I have heard it asserted by some that America hath flourished under her connection from Great Britain," he wrote. "Their attachment to Britain (is) obstinate, and it (is) a kind of treason to speak against it. Their ideas for grievance (operate) without resentment and their single object (is) reconciliation."

The grievances laid out against Britain were based upon a desire among revolutionaries to wipe out the old order and replace it with the new. Still, Paine's propaganda had been effective enough.

"Without the pen of the author of *Common Sense*, the sword of Washington would have been raised in vain," remarked John Adams, who served as the first Vice President and second President of the United States. Paine's vision, he said, "was so democratic, without any restraint or even an attempt at any equilibrium or counter poise, that it must produce confusion and every evil work."

Reflecting his interest in revolution for its own sake, Paine compared the colonies to a "child (who) has thrived on milk, that is never to have meat," or to a people who believed that the first 20 years of their lives must necessarily be like the next 20. "The authority of Great Britain over this continent is a form of government which sooner or later must end," he wrote without providing a single compelling reason.

Paine's writings were directed at the "divine right of kings" which stood in the way of Venetian designs to usurp power from the British Monarchy. "Under how many subtitles or absurdities has the divine right to govern been imposed on the credulity of mankind," Paine fumed.

While gunning for revolution, Paine acknowledged that "the government seems to be placating its need for a foe; for unless it finds one somewhere, no *pretext* exists for the enormous revenue and taxation now deemed necessary." In other words, shadowy interests needed the excuse of war to generate revenue for their private enterprises. With the East India Company relying heavily on funding from the British Parliament to expand its operations in the colonies and around the world and to fund its armies, the international bankers and Venetian merchants needed a pretext for war.

In the end, the American Revolution proved so draining on British financial reserves that it forced the British government to double taxes, thereby increasing disquiet among the Britons against their own government while undercutting public support for the British and colonial governments, rendering them more vulnerable to coups.

As revolutionaries, the shadow elites promoted notions of "a living Constitution" and "living *Bible*" that could be reinterpreted over and over again to establish grievances that could be exploited for private gain. Paine even wrote that a law that was valid one day could be interpreted as invalid the next. For example, a law written before a child was even born is necessarily oppressive, he argued, as the child never had a chance to weigh in on its merits or agree to be legally bound by the law before the law was imposed upon him. Therefore all societies are necessarily unjust and undemocratic since not every person has had a chance to weigh in on every law.

To foment unrest, the Venetians sought to indoctrinate the child into values that supported a new order and pitted him against the values of his parents and society to give him cause to rebel. "The circumstances of the world are continually changing, and the opinions of men change also; and as the government is for the living, and not for the dead, it is the living only that has any right to it," Paine wrote. "That which may be thought right and found convenient in one age may be thought wrong and found inconvenient in another. In such cases, who is to decide, the living or the dead?"

In contrast, righteous colonists sought to instill morals, values and traditions in their children that they could pass down from one generation to the next. Children would look to their parents as role models and aspire to be like them while parents helped mold them into responsible adults who would carry on the family name and legacy. In this way, a society, culture, and tradition are formed around a shared history, values, and expectations. There was a natural order of things. Parents cared for their children, and in their old age, the children would look after their parents, who helped pass on values, wisdom, and wealth to the next generation.

However, for the Venetians, stability stood in the way of change, and so they stoked rebellion whenever possible. Oppression, they argued, was a natural state of affairs, and therefore revolution was always justified. If an invading force were to enter a country of established traditions and hierarchies, the invaders would necessarily be placed at an unfair advantage against others whose families and hierarchies had lived there for generations. A revolution would therefore be justified to overthrow the existing order in the interests of "democracy and fairness." Change agents therefore looked for or created underdogs and victims who could be enlisted to their cause to overthrow the status quo. "That which is called aristocracy in some countries and nobility in others arose out of the governments founded upon conquest," Paine stated, nursing resentments based upon the politics of envy.

Old orders and existing values could be torn down through public ridicule, Paine wrote. "If a whole country is disposed to hold (leaders) in contempt, all their value is gone, and one will own them. It is common opinion only that makes them anything, or nothing, or worse than nothing. There is no occasion to take titles away for they take themselves away when society concurs to ridicule them." Among the Venetian's favorite targets for ridicule was religion. Mockery was a strategy the Venetians used to undermine the power of nations and their leaders for the purposes of conquest, thereby giving rise to the endless mockery rife throughout modern political discourse. Not unsurprisingly, ridicule became a "rule" in Saul Alinsky's *Rules for Radicals,* that modern revolutionaries used to upset the existing order.

From the vantage point of "enlightened" thinkers, religion was irrational and based upon superstition. Virtue and morals stood in the way of rational self-interest, empire building, and plunder. Without moral constraints, man could be reduced to a savage and psychopath for whom any vice could be justified in the pursuit of personal gain. The Venetian empire builders therefore rejected a belief of God – and any other authority higher than themselves. If Jesus could be the son of God and a God himself, then the Venetian oligarchs could elevate themselves to the status of Gods. If they were to become as Gods, through what they considered to be their superior intelligence and black magic, then the people, who were their subjects, deserved to be oppressed, exploited, and disposed of at will. The people's plight was deserved, the Enlightened philosophers concluded, by virtue of their own naivete and trust in the goodness of mankind. Aristotle, a classical Greek philosopher whose ideas inspired the rational Enlightenment, even went so far as to claim that people lacked souls and that they could be programmed to think and do as instructed by elites.

The agenda behind the Enlightenment was not the liberation of conscience, but the liberation from conscience, which is enslavement. Revolution provided a pretext to challenge the "divine right to rule" to usurp the power of Christian Monarchs, not create democratic governments that answered to the people; they sought to sweep away an old guard so that a tyrannical ruler could emerge in its place. As the Marquis de Condorcet, a mathematician, said of the Enlightenment, its proponents were "a class of men less concerned with discovering the truth than propagating it."

The influence of the Venetians in the U.S. Constitution can be seen in the separation of powers doctrine. Enlightened philosophers argued that freedom could only be exercised through a regime whose laws were enacted by an elected legislature, administered by a separate executive, and enforced by an independent judiciary, based upon the concept of the Venetian republic in which democracy was merely an illusion and real power was held by the oligarchs. The real purpose of checks and balances was to check the power of the King and enable the merchant-warrior class to ascend through the ranks and then consolidate its power within the government. The American government was not set up as a pure democracy, but as a republic in which, through successive political cycles, corporate interests would increase their control over the separate branches of government to the point where they now move in lockstep with each other and serve the interests of a shadow elite at the expense of the people. The government was created and shaped this way by design and was only representative of the people for as long as its people remained virtuous and had the spark of liberty and God within their hearts, creating what was known throughout the world as "American exceptionalism."

Venice was known as the "Serene Republic," which perpetrated oligarchical rule from the fifteenth century onward. The Venetians oligarchy was described in Plato's *Republic* as having "a constitution according to property, in which the rich govern, and the poor has no share in government." The shadow elite maintain control through oppression and terror as part of a strategy to subdue and demoralize. Their government is hereditary and dynastic, resembling what the America's government has become today, with the Bush, Kennedy, and Clinton dynasties dominating the political scene. Materialistic at its core, the Enlightened ideas espoused by Adam Smith, a Scottish economist, philosopher, and pioneer of political economy, argued that, "the desire to grow rich is as natural in us as the desire to live....Nature provides the brute animals with the things necessary for their lives, but in man, whom it makes poor, naked, and subject to many needs, it inserts this desire for riches and gives him the intelligence and industry to acquire them." The Enlightened ones, or Illuminati, sought to accumulate wealth and power above all else.

The American government is now in the hands of oligarchs who have created a self-perpetuating elite who promote public looting and reinforce power and privilege for a select few at the expense of the many. Their philosophy is Aristotelian at his premise – one that rejects God and the existence of a soul and reinforces a belief that there is a class of rulers and a class of ruled, with the latter serving as slaves who are stripped of their rights, wealth, and dignity. Power is to be set aside for select families and passed on arbitrarily through bloodlines, regardless of ability or character. Creativity and scientific discovery were replaced with plagiarism, pseudo-science, false doctrines, and expertise that could not be questioned.

After Thomas Paine released his pamphlets, Adam Weishaupt, a Professor of Canon Law from the electorate of Bavaria, founded the Order of the Illuminati on May 1, 1776. A student of the rational Enlightenment, Weishaupt believed that he was destined to bring the Antichrist to power.

Weishaupt created a private occult, the Golden Dawn, as a cover for the Venetian agenda which was founded by the Society of Jesus (Jesuits), the largest Roman Catholic religious order led by the Black Pope (Jesuit Superior General). After Weishaupt's father died, he lived with his godfather, Baron Johann Van Ickstaff, a proponent of the rational Enlightenment. Based upon the Knights Templar and Jesuits, this new secret society enabled members to grow wealthy and powerful through political intrigue, assassinations, and random acts of opportunism stripped of morality.

Weishaupt's new order was linked into a network of spies and informants, based upon the Venetian spy model, which secretly provided them raw, timely intelligence.

While Weishaupt was establishing his secret society, Thomas Jefferson wrote the *Declaration of Independence*, which was adopted by the Second Continental Congress in Philadelphia, Pennsylvania on July 4, 1776.

The *Declaration* was a manifesto that was written to explain why the thirteen colonies were at war with Great Britain. The *Declaration* was described as a work of genius as it's elegantly written and simply worded, a clear declaration of grievances against the British Crown, which drew a proverbial line in the sand that signaled the colonists' desire to separate from England.

The King appointed John Lind, an English politician, to review the document. Lind, in turn, wrote a rather clunky, well reasoned response to the points raised. No doubt his response was tossed into the bin without so much as a second thought as the revolutionaries had already made up their minds that they wanted the separation, just as the neoconservatives decided that they wanted to wage war against Iraq regardless of the well-reasoned reservations others had.

Lind characterized Jefferson's *Declaration* as "a cloud of words." On its face, Jefferson's often quoted preamble is ludicrous and hypocritical, Lind observed. As Jefferson wrote: "We hold these truths to be self-evident, that all men are created equal, that they are endowed by their Creator with certain unalienable rights, that among these are life, liberty, and the pursuit of happiness. That, to secure these rights, governments are instituted among men, deriving their just powers from the consent of the governed. That, whenever any form of government becomes destructive of these ends, it is the right of the people to alter or to abolish it, and to institute a new government, laying its foundation on such principles, and organizing its powers in such form, as to them shall seem most likely to effect their safety and happiness."

When Jefferson wrote these words, he was a slave owner. Not only did Jefferson own slaves, but he was charged with raping one of them, a 13-year-old girl by the name of Sally Hemmings, making him an accused pedophile. That Jefferson was a slave owner is not surprising given that the East India Company was then engaged in human trafficking. The Venetians and their agents, like the Rothschilds, were also bankrolling revolutionaries, like Jefferson. Most colonialists and British agents opposed slavery at a time when revolutionaries were preaching liberty, fraternity, and equality. Those same revolutionaries were actually slave owners.

Parliament outlawed slavery in 1807.

While characterizing the revolutionaries as "fanatics" who were outright fabricating grievances in order to justify their rebellion, Lind observed that the revolutionaries had taken life, liberty, and property from others. How could they champion principles they did not themselves believe or practice?

Based upon the *Declaration*, Lind concluded, thieves could not be restrained from thieving, murderers were free to murder, and rebels were given license to overthrow governments. The document, he said, "put an ax to the root of all government, yet in the same breath talks of government."

The public was not even allowed to weigh in on the merits, Lind wrote, characterizing Jefferson as "treasonous" and part of "a nefarious scheme." As Lind observed, while filing grievances against Britain, the revolutionaries set fire to British boats, blocked British trade, and directed Indians to fight against British troops on American soil. In other words, the revolutionaries were the instigators.

While agents of the Enlightenment were stirring up revolution among the colonies, others were stirring up revolution in France. As could be observed, wealthy aristocrats were bankrolling revolution on behalf of "the people." For example, a wealthy French patrician by the name of Jacques Donatren Le Ray de Chaumont helped finance the American Revolution and broker talks between French King Louis XVI and colonial representatives. He aligned the American colonies and France against Britain at the prompting of Ben Franklin in the interests of acquiring more land in North America for the French. As a dutiful agent of change, Franklin was gifted a palatial Parisian home by de Chaumont. While French revolutionaries took up the cause of liberty, fraternity, and equality, Franklin spent his days in Paris canoodling with French courtesans, indulging in fine Parisian foods, and deafening his conscience with unrestrained decadence.

Once the American Revolution got underway, Weishaupt was initiated into the Masonic lodge where he announced a plan to subvert and overthrow governments around the world through secret fellowships and networks working on behalf of a secret shadow elite.

The Freemasons would continue to recruit good and influential men into their ranks who believed in the traditions of service and charity. They expected to network with fellow members to promote their careers and serve their communities, not understanding the nature of the order they had joined until they had progressed well through its ranks. At its core, Freemasonry espoused the principles of the rational Enlightenment by promoting "illumination, enlightening the understanding by the sun of reason, which will dispel the clouds of superstition and prejudice."

General George Washington, who led a colonial army into war against Great Britain, was elected first President of the United States. His writings reflect that he was aware and concerned about the events unfolding around him. Despite being a Freemason, Washington appears to have been a man of principle who loved his country and feared God. He is remembered as the President who could not tell a lie.

While Washington inherited 10 slaves upon the death of his father and purchased dozens more over the course of his life – and even supported a measure passed by Congress to protect the institution of slavery, he confessed to his private secretary that he found slavery repugnant and made arrangements to free his slaves upon his death. That he and his family had slaves in the first place was no doubt a product of his affiliation with the East India Company that trafficked them and enlisted him to fight in the American Revolution. As he matured and consulted his conscience, Washington acknowledged the evils of the institution. Unlike his compatriots, he was not convinced of the merits of the Enlightenment and retained his faith in God.

Washington was plain spoken and honest. Before the Battle of Long Island in 1776, Washington told the Continental Army: "The time is now near at hand which must probably determine whether Americans are to be freemen or slaves; whether they are to have any property they can call their own; whether their houses and farms are to be pillaged and destroyed, and themselves consigned to a state of wretchedness from which no human efforts will deliver them. The fate of unborn millions will now depend, under God, on the courage and conduct of this army. Our cruel and unrelenting enemy leaves us only the choice of brave resistance, or the most abject submission. We have, therefore, to resolve to conquer or die."

The enemy was clearly not the Monarch but the shadow rulers who sought to enslave mankind and plunder the assets of the British Empire and its colonies. The fight was therefore for dominance which would allow the country to take control of its own destiny as foreign forces coalesced around it. Many patriots were aware of the traitors from within.

Thanks to the wisdom of Washington and others, the United States was founded as a country of, by, and for a free people under God. Washington was the right man at the right time. Wise to the wiles of the old world and appreciating the rare opportunity the Founding Fathers had for American exceptionalism, he proceeded cautiously and with vigilance, ensuring that the reach of the shadow elite was kept at bay. The Founding Fathers had secured liberty for Americans. It was now up to Americans to keep it.

Washington warned about the shadow foreign powers in his Farewell Address, which he delivered before retiring to Mount Vernon, Virginia. Washington wisely enjoined morality with freedom, explaining that one cannot exist without the other: "Of all the dispositions and habits which lead to political prosperity, religion and morality are indispensable supports. In vain would that man claim the tribute of patriotism, who should labor to subvert these great pillars of human happiness, these firmest props of the duties of men and citizens. The mere politician, equally with the pious man, ought to respect and to cherish them. A volume could not trace all their connections with private and public felicity. Let it simply be asked: Where is the security for property, for reputation, for life, if the sense of religious obligation desert the oaths which are the instruments of investigation in courts of justice? And let us with caution indulge the supposition that morality can be maintained without religion. Whatever may be conceded to the influence of refined education on minds of peculiar structure, reason and experience both forbid us to expect that national morality can prevail in exclusion of religious principle."

While the Venetians and their agents lurked in the shadows of America, Washington reminded his countrymen to "observe good faith and justice towards all nations; cultivate peace and harmony with all.... It will be worthy of a free, enlightened, and at no distant period, a great nation, to give to mankind the magnanimous and too novel example of a people always guided by an exalted justice and benevolence.... The experiment, at least, is recommended by every sentiment which ennobles human nature. Alas! is it rendered impossible by its vices.... Against the insidious wiles of foreign influence ... the jealousy of a free people ought to be constantly awake, since history and experience prove that foreign influence is one of the most baneful foes of republican government....The great rule of conduct for us in regard to foreign nations is in extending our commercial relations, to have with them as little political connection as possible. So far as we have already formed engagements, let them be fulfilled with perfect good faith. Here let us stop. Europe has a set of primary interests which to us have none; or a very remote relation. Hence she must be engaged in frequent controversies, the causes of which are essentially foreign to our concerns. Hence, therefore, it must be unwise in us to implicate ourselves by artificial ties in the ordinary vicissitudes of her politics, or the ordinary combinations and collisions of her friendships or enmities. Our detached and distant situation invites and enables us to pursue a different course....Why forego the advantages of so peculiar a situation? Why quit our own to stand upon foreign ground? Why, by interweaving our destiny with that of any part of Europe, entangle our peace and prosperity in the toils of European ambition, rivalship, interest, humor, or caprice?"

Once Thomas Paine returned to England, a warrant was issued for his arrest, leading him to flee to French where he was elected to the French National Convention to support the Jacobins who demanded revolution and an end to the French Monarchy. During the Jacobin movement, a Reign of Terror was unleashed upon the French nation that resulted in the arrest and execution of over 10,000 people. The motto of the Jacobin Club was "Vivre libre ou mo" ("live free or die").

Paine authored the *Rights of Man* in defense of the French Revolution, but British Prime Minister William Pitt the Younger suppressed Paine's works in Britain, lest his radicalism spread there.

The French Revolution began in May of 1789 when the Ancien Régime was abolished in favor of a constitutional monarchy, the First French Republic, which was established in 1792. King Louis XVI who supported the American Revolution, expecting that France could claim land through the war, was executed.

Upon being questioned about the King's execution, Paine said that the French Revolution wasn't directed against King Louis XVI, but against the "despotic principles of the Government," which did not originate from the King but from "the original establishment, many centuries back which were too deeply rooted to be removed." While paying lip service to liberty, fraternity, and equality, the revolution served the purpose of clearing out a class of nobles so that a rival faction could seize their assets and replace them.

Revolutions were part of a war strategy to uproot, re-envision, and re-imagine society before disrupting it again and again until its values and principles were aligned with those that served and reinforced the power of a secret ruling elite, who pursued what Paine called "universal revolution." Paine clarified that "every office and department has its despotism, founded upon custom and usage. Every place has its Bastille, and every Bastille has its despot."

The "storming of the Bastille," or political prison, occurred in Revolutionary France on July 14, 1790, representing an attack on the institution of the Monarchy. Revolutionaries always appealed to universal values – that of equality, liberty, and fraternity -- while betraying these very principles.

As the merchants of Venice understood, war generated profits for merchants and debt for governments, which resulted in taxes, which created grievances, which led to revolutions that cleared out an old guard to make way for the new. At the same time, international financiers who bankrolled the debt were able to exert control over the new government and redirect the public's wealth to themselves under the pretext of helping the people.

To cite one example, revolutionaries directed King Louis XIV to lend financial support to help the colonists fight the American Revolution so that France could advance through Britain's retreat. The debt accrued through this war bankrupted the French government. When a drought created a famine, the French Treasury was unable to subsidize flour to prevent mass starvation, creating the conditions for the French Revolution, with resulted in the King's execution. The new French Revolutionary government seized Le Ray de Chaumont's assets and Chateau at Chaumont-sur-Loire after he financed the American Revolution, with Ben Franklin's support. The revolution then set the stage for Napoleon Bonaparte to emerge as French dictator. So much for life, liberty, and equality.

Before, during, and after the American Revolution, Venetian collaborators were placed into key positions of power. Many, like Franklin, assumed ambassadorships. Another Venetian agent, Thomas Jefferson, succeeded Washington as leader of the nation.

As President, Jefferson appointed James Monroe as special envoy. In this role, Monroe negotiated Paine's release from a

Parisian prison and doubled the size of the United States with the Louisiana Purchase.

After the American Revolution, America fell into debt, rendering the country vulnerable to take over by the bankers. The nation's first Treasury Secretary, Alexander Hamilton, launched the first Bank of the United States as a central bank that enabled the Rothschilds to control America's money supply. The bank's charter expired in 1811.

Vigilant patriots who understood that a central bank imperiled the country's independence and the people's freedom refused to renew the bank's charter. Once the charter ended, the War of 1812 broke out, with Andrew Jackson characterizing it as "a Banker's War." Once he became President, Jackson immediately paid off the national debt and refused to sign a charter for a new central bank. "I am one of those who do not believe that a national debt is a national blessing but rather a curse to a republic; in as much as it is calculated to raise around the Administration a monied aristocracy dangerous to the liberties of the country." The bankers retaliated by attempting to assassinate Jackson, who called them "a den of vipers and thieves (whom) I intend to rout out."

The Civil War broke out two decades later, pitting the nation against itself and placing the country back into debt to the Rothschilds who financed both sides. Seventy-seven years later, the Federal Reserve was established, forming a permanent Central Bank that allowed private bankers control of the nation's money supply, and ultimately, its policy, so that they could manipulate the "representative government" into serving a shadow elite at the expense of the people.

II.
Caesar's Palace

Rome was not built in a day, but the first brick was laid with the birth of Jesus Christ. In the 6th century, an Italian monk by the name of St. Dionysius Exiguus conceived the idea to use the time stamp "BC" to refer to the period before Christ and "AD" to refer to Ammo Domini, or the "Year of our Lord," establishing new time stamps for the Gregorian and Christianized Julian Calendars. According to Royal insiders, Jesus survived the crucifixion to sire a child who was then adopted into the Roman ruling families in exchange for imparting his knowledge of the Egyptian mystery schools, thus establishing the "divine rite to rule." Whether or not Jesus passed on his genetic heritage is an exploration for a different book. Suffice to say, his spiritual teachings, life, and impact were sufficiently influential to have transformed society forever, with ministers, rulers, people of all trades and walks of life inspired to follow him and become initiated into this new religion. Through Jesus and his disciples, God's word spread throughout the land. Churches played organ music that transmitted sounds whose vibrations healed the bodies, minds, and souls of those who heard it. Singing in choir became a way to celebrate God and lift the spirit. Jesus imparted not only a moral code but worked with energies to heal, inspire, and elevate humanity, moving society away from the barbarism of the past to civility.

William Shakespeare's *Tragedy of Julius Caesar* depicts the moral challenges facing Julius Caesar, the Republic of Rome's last dictator. As Caesar tried to reform society and extend rights and privileges to the people, he faced aggressive push-back from patricians. In 60 BC, Caesar formed the First Triumvirate within the Roman Senate to challenge the patricians' monopoly on power. Despite having been born into a patrician family himself, Caesar understood that a stable and just society must represent the interests of the people and treat them fairly. To this end, Caesar instituted democratic reforms and expanded protections and privileges for ordinary people. With the public rallying around him, Caesar inspired loving devotion from the electorate and burning resentment from elites.

As a young man, Caesar impressed others as an able military general, charismatic public speaker, gifted strategist, and natural leader. Through his exploits, he caught the attention of the ruling classes. As he racked up military victories, elites agreed to fund his political campaign for Pontifex Maximum (Chief Priest), a position he handily won in 60 BC. Under Caesar's leadership, Rome's wealth and land holdings increased. Caesar went on to conquer Gaul and Spain and then invaded England. As the ruling class celebrated Caesar's service to Rome, Marcus Antonious (Mark Antony) attempted three times to crown him King. Caesar humbly refused each time, leading others to believe that he was truly a man of the people.

His rivals were of a different disposition, however.

Jealous of Caesar's newfound power and popularity, they sabotaged the ruler at every turn. One can imagine that Caesar felt much like President Donald Trump who was attempting to establish a government that truly reflected the will of the people only to be backstabbed and frustrated. With enemies encircling him, Caesar imposed martial law to maintain order, leading to charges that he was a self-aggrandizing dictator. During one of his campaigns, he invaded the royal palace of Egypt and helped restore Cleopatra to the throne.

Cleopatra was a powerful ruler in her own right. After an affair, she lobbied Caesar to adopt their son so that he would become an heir to the Roman Empire. Caesar rejected her entreaties and chose his own grand nephew, Ocatvius Thurinus (Caesar Augustus), instead.

Caesar maintained the courage of his convictions throughout. "Cowards die many times before their deaths; the valiant never taste of death but once," Caesar proclaimed in *The Tragedy of Julius Caesar.* Caesar rejected political expediency in the interests of doing what he thought was right. For example, he whittled away the power of the patricians, redistributed property to the poor, reformed the tax system, rebuilt Carthage, and shared Rome's prosperity with his constituents. So great was Caesar's impact that he was named Dictator Perpetuus (dictator for life).

As Caesar's power and reputation grew, patricians raised concerns that he would abolish the Senate entirely, so they plotted his assassination, a tragedy Shakespeare depicted in *The Tragedy of Julius Caesar.*

Among Caesar's assassins was Brutus, an heir.

"Et tu, Brute (Brutus)?" a betrayed Caesar asked in his dying breath as his body was punctured with the knives.

Caesar died having been betrayed by his closest advisors.

In an effort to claim Rome for themselves, Mark Antony and Cleopatra teamed up and declared war against Caesar Augustus, who handily defeated them in battle. Caesar had judged Cleopatra well. Like other patricians, she was concerned principally with her own power. Caesar Augustus went on to establish the Roman Principate, the first phase of the Roman Empire. Addressing Romans at Caesar's funeral, Mark Anthony spoke to the greatness of Caesar and his closely guarded admiration for the fallen ruler:

Friends, Romans, countrymen, lend me your ears
I come to bury Caesar, not to praise him
The evil that men do lives after them
The good is oft interred with their bones
So let it be with Caesar

The noble Brutus hath told you Caesar was ambitious
If it were so, it was a grievous fault
And grievously hath Caesar answered it
Here, under leave of Brutus and the rest
(For Brutus is an honourable man
So are they all; all honourable men)
Come I to speak in Caesar's funeral

He was my friend, faithful and just to me
But Brutus says he was ambitious

And Brutus is an honourable man

He hath brought many captives home to Rome
Whose ransoms did the general coffers fill
Did this in Caesar seem ambitious
When that the poor have cried, Caesar hath wept
Ambition should be made of sterner stuff
Yet Brutus says he was ambitious
And Brutus is an honourable man

You all did see that on the Lupercal
I thrice presented him a kingly crown
Which he did thrice refuse: was this ambition
Yet Brutus, he is an honourable man

I speak not to disprove what Brutus spoke
But here I am to speak what I do know
You all did love him once, not without cause
What cause withholds you then to mourn for him

O judgment! Thou art fled to brutish beasts
And men have lost their reason.... Bear with me
My heart is in the coffin there with Caesar
And I must pause till it comes back to me

Jesus' influence had taken root among the ruling classes, inspiring them to understand that God's will was for people to serve each other and serve God, to live honorably and justly rather than dedicating oneself to vain self-aggrandizement, plunder, and barbarous murders. Reflecting the influence of Jesus, Caesar Augustus declared himself to be the son of God.

All Roads Lead to Rome

In the early days of the Roman Empire, Christians were

persecuted. Yet, their faith endured. One Emperor, Nero, was reported to have killed and tortured Christians and thrown them to the dogs. Some he set on fire. Despite the abuse inflicted upon them, Christianity continued to spread.

Among the most notable Christian Roman rulers was Constantine the Great. In 313 AD, Roman Emperor Constantine issued the Edict of Milan, which legalized the public practice of Christianity. He also convened the Council of Nicaea, an ecumenical council which gathered Christian leaders together to establish a formal understanding of Christian orthodoxy, resulting in the Nicene Creed. At the same time, he discouraged paganism.

"By keeping the divine faith, I am made a partaker of the light of truth," Constantine wrote in a letter to the King of Persians in 333. "I advance in the knowledge of the divine faith.... This God I invoke with bended knees. (I) recoil with horror from the blood of sacrifices from their foul and detestable odors and from every earth-born magic fire for the profane and impious superstitions which are defiled by these rites have cast down and consigned to perdition many, nay, whole nations of the gentile world."

In 330 AD, Constantine wrote to the Numidian bishops: "The will of the Supreme God, who is the author of this world and its Father, that the whole human race should agree together and be joined in a certain affectionate union by, as it were, a mutual embrace."

Under Constantine's rule, Jews and Christians lived together amicably as brothers, sisters, friends, and colleagues. At the same time, Jews were not allowed to enslave Christians. On Constantine's orders, the Church of the Holy Sepulchre was built on Jesus' tomb in Jerusalem, and basilicas sprouted up throughout the Roman Empire. Constantine also lowered taxes for clergy who devoted their lives to religious service and recruited righteous Romans who had faithfully served in the church to join his government.

During his reign, Constantine returned property stolen from Christians, approved the construction of Old Saint Peter's Basilica on St. Peter's resting place at the Vatican, ensured that Christians were not legally required to participate in pagan blood sacrifices, and replaced pagan symbols with Christian marks on Roman coins. Constantine went on to establish the City of Constantinople (now Istanbul) as the new capitol of the Roman Empire and a vibrant center for Christian activity.

By 380 AD, Emperor Theodosius issued the *Edict of Thessalonica* which made Christianity the official religion of the Roman Empire. Once paganism spread, fault lines appeared throughout the Roman Empire, causing it to crumble. Within decades, the Roman Empire split in two, with the Byzantine Empire forming the east and the Holy Roman Empire forming in the west. And then came the hordes.

In 410, Rome was sacked by Visigoths, an early Germanic people whom Julius Caesar had previous pushed back and whose symbol was the eagle. Wave after wave of nomadic tribes began to migrate into the Roman Empire in what was known as the invasion of the barbarians. The barbarians were often pagans and involved in the occult. Appreciating the threat they posed, the Romans attempted to Christianize them with mixed results.

As Romans raised concerns that their Gods were punishing them for accepting Christianity, a Christian apologist by the name of St. Augustine of Hippo defended the faith. Far from rendering Rome vulnerable, he said, Christianity had fortified the Empire. St.

Augustine reminded the Romans that slavery was an abomination to God and that slaves should be freed as an "act of piety." He also encouraged rulers to establish laws against slave traders and to outlaw child trafficking. "The condition of slavery is the result of sin," he wrote in *The City of God.* "The lowly position does as much good to the servant as the proud position does harm to the master."

At the same time, he counseled slaves to humbly accept their lot in life "not in crafty fear, but in faithful love" until slavery could be abolished altogether. "Thus, a good man, though a slave, is free; but a wicked man, though a King, is a slave."

St. Augustine also cautioned Romans against harming Jews, stating, "slay them not, lest they should at last forget (God's) law."

Rather, Jews should be free to live in Christian lands unharmed.

Romans, he said, should cultivate discernment and arm themselves with the shield of God to protect themselves, their families, and the Empire from harm. "There are wolves within, and there are sheep without," Augustine wrote. "What is a kingdoms without justice – they're just gangs of bandits."

Despite the temptation to act in kind, St. Augustine encouraged Romans not to abandon their faith or answer the call of the decadent occultists: "He that becomes protector of sin shall surely become its prisoner. The Devil would not ... tempt man into doing something which God has forbidden, had man not already begun to seek satisfaction in himself, and, consequently, to take pleasure in the words: 'You shall be as God,' The promise of these words, however, would much more truly have come to pass if, by obedience, Adam and Eve had kept close to the ultimate and true Source of their being and had not, by pride, imagined that they were themselves the source of their being. For, created gods are gods not in virtue of their own being but by a participation in the being of the true God. For, whoever seeks to be more than he is becomes less, and while he aspires to be self-sufficing he retires from Him who is truly sufficient for him."

Bloody Barbarians

The Republic of Venice was once among the most pious of places in all of Europe. The Lagoon was known for its strict morality until it suffered recurring invasions from warring hordes, including an attack by Attila the Hun in 340. Beautiful Venice, with is canals and ports, was a perfect outpost for trade – and lure for merchants who envisioned they could expand their markets and amass more wealth by partnering with mercenary forces who could forge new trade routes and plunder. As the hordes flooded into Venice, the God-fearing fled. Venice then fell to the Byzantine Empire only to claimed by Gothic Kings and reclaimed by the Byzantines again. Soon a warrior-merchant class, who professed to be Christian, came to dominate the Venetian Lagoon.

In the 6th century, while Venice was under Byzantine control, a semi-nomadic, Turkic-speaking tribe called the Khazars established a commercial empire covering the southeastern section of what is now modern Europe, Russia, southern Ukraine, Crimea and Kazakhstan. While the original Byzantine leaders were Christians, the Khazars practiced black magic. As they traveled from one destination to the next, they ruthlessly killed people and seized their assets. In an effort to curtail their relentless barbarism, the European rulers gave the Khazars an ultimatum – either convert to Christianity, Judaism, or Islam or face extermination. The Khazars decided to "convert" to Judaism, concluding that Christians had their own kingdoms; the Muslims had a caliphate; and the Jews were a disbursed people. By adopting Judaism, they hoped to conquer and establish their own kingdom under this religion, even though they privately rejected Judaism.

Like many nomadic warrior tribes who traversed the Eurasian continent, the Khazars were messianic and embraced different religions at different times, fluidly assuming one religious identify after another. They rejected Jesus, but embraced the idea of a messiah, who was to establish a kingdom in keeping with the traditions of Christian rulers who ruled by "divine rite," only theirs would be a warrior-king and an Antichrist. They considered themselves to have received a mandate from the Heavens to rule over others.

Judah Halevi, a Khazarian living in Spain in the 11th century, encouraged the nomadic tribes to embrace messianism. Another Khazar, David Alroy, who was born in Amadiya, Iraq under the name of Menahem ben Soloman, dabbled in the black arts. After convincing others that he was the long awaited Messiah, Alroy directed his followers to attack Amadiya as fictitious Talmudic scholars. Once the warriors gained access to the city, they planned to pull swords from their long robes and kill their hosts. Word traveled fast, preventing Alroy and his followers from unleashing mayhem on the city.

Byzantine rulers aligned with the Pope against the Seljuk

Turks, who served as mercenaries in Khazar armies while the Khazars were attempting to stake claim on Jerusalem for the "Jews." The Turks often identified with Islam.

Pope Urban II launched the First Crusade, establishing the Latin Kingdom of Jerusalem for "Christianity" after Constantine established the Church of the Holy Sepulchre in Jerusalem. At the same time, Muslims were advancing into the Holy Land. By claiming Jerusalem for the "Jews," the Khazars attempted to establish a dominant position there. Several crusades followed which were launched by powerful merchants using religion as a vehicle for conquest. The Knights Templar offered protection to Pilgrims en route to Jerusalem to secure trade routes and plunder wealth for the Venetians.

As various religious factious vied for control of Jerusalem, a council was held at the Church of the Holy Sepulchre to establish the Kingdom of Jerusalem as a theocratic state under papal control. The Byzantine Empire then established an alliance with the Kingdom of Jerusalem. After Constantinople became a destination for Italian merchants and Crusaders en route to the Holy Land, the Venetians, the Genoese, and other traders opened up ports on the Aegean Sea for commerce in which goods were shipped to Byzantium via Constantinople.

Once the Kingdom of Jerusalem fell, another Crusade was launched, thus re-establishing the Kingdom. Dominated by the Italian city states of Venice and Genoa, the Kingdom of Jerusalem remained a target for the imperial designs of the shadow elite and merchant-warrior classes. If religion legitimized power, the shadow elite sought to rule the world from the holy city. If these usurpers could fulfill prophecy by establishing a kingdom for the "Jews," even if they had to make false assertions to this end, then Christian Europe would have to accept their authority. However, the real Jews, who followed the covenant, were promised their own homeland through divine providence not warrior diplomacy.

By the 13th century, the Mongols, who served as Venice's mercenary army unsuccessfully attempted to conquer Jerusalem. At the same time, the Venetians acquired trading privileges with the

Byzantine Empire whose merchants ships were supported by a powerful navy.

As the hordes rushed in, the Byzantine Empire went through a rapid succession of incompetent, corrupt rulers. In 1183, Andronikos Komnenos became Byzantine Emperor by seizing the throne. He then marched into Constantinople, seized Venetian property, and imprisoned its owners only to be taken captive by the Khazarian Seljuq Turks. Upon his release, he attempted to assassinate the aristocrats and implant his grandson as King of Jerusalem. The desire to claim Jerusalem was based upon commercial, not religious imperatives.

The Khazars served in armies for the Muslim caliphate, the Byzantine Empire, and the Venetian Empire whose merchants became quite wealthy, with many found to be in possession of prized jewels and treasures acquired through their adventures in plunder and pillage. It would not be long before the Byzantine emperors established alliances and intermarried with the Khazars. One Byzantine emperor, Leo III, arranged for his son, Constantine, to marry a Khazar princess, Tzitzak (Irene), to formalize an alliance between the two empires. Their son, Leo IV, was known as Leo the Khazar. As military general, Constantine solidified his empire's borders and expanded them to the East and West.

Under Khazarian rule, Christianity was under assault from all directions. The Khazars forbade prayer and were fierce iconoclasts, who rejected any depictions of Christ as idolatry. Historians characterized Leo as a "monster athirst for blood," "a ferocious beast," "an unclean and bloodstained magician taking pleasure in evoking demons," and an "Antichrist." This same man was described by his Khazar supporters as a "victorious and prophetic Emperor." While banning the "cult of saints" as idolatrous, his subjects were expected to idolize him as if he were a God.

Living under Khazar rule was so unbearable that Roman citizens gathered in Constantinople to demand that their Emperor convert to Orthodox Christianity. Meanwhile the Byzantines endured recurring invasions from nomadic tribes and barbarians. In time, the entire Byzantine Empire began to take on a warlike quality itself, eventually establishing a marauding army that sought to conquer behind a Christian shield. And then came the pretenders to the throne.

As barbarians overtook the empire, rulers brutalized and back-stabbed each other. At the same time, they mismanaged their societies, squandered their wealth, and aspired to live the opulent lifestyle of Kings as effete aristocrats. Many falsely claimed to be descendants of great Roman Emperors who were Christians while flouting Christian virtues.

While maintaining a public face of Christianity, the rulers embraced a death cult associated with shamanism and black magic. Among their practices was iconoclasm – that is, forbidding the veneration or artistic depictions (in statues or paintings) of religious icons on grounds that such images constituted idolatry. Christians enjoyed paintings and statues of Jesus, the disciples, among other Christian icons. They didn't worship these images, but were inspired by them.

As black magicians, occultists understood the power of imagery. Since rulers steeped in the occult wished to be worshiped, they replaced Christian images with images of themselves, reflecting that their iconoclasm was not rooted in preventing idol worship but in encouraging idol worship of themselves. Christian images were therefore replaced with images of the occult.

Once the Khazars solidified their control of the Byzantine Empire, the Empire fell to perpetual war and eventual ruin.

By the eighth century, Venice, which was part of the Byzantine Empire, elected its first Doge. Merchants traveled the Eurasian continent seeking new markets, including Marco Polo who made his way through Asia along the Silk Road. Through his travels, Venetian merchants established lucrative trade routes and recruited mercenaries to accompany them on journeys of pillage and plunder.

When word got out about the barbarism of the mercenaries, Marco Polo mollified Christian by perpetuating the myth of Prester John. A descendant of the Three Magi, Prester John, was said to have presided over a kingdom filled with magic, incredible wealth, and mythological creatures. The warrior king was reputed to have saved the Holy Land from Muslim infidels and pagans by savagely butchering them. When word of the barbarian savagery circulated around Judeo-Christian Europe, ordinary people would dismiss it as fantasy or as part of a holy war defending Christian faith in a far off, distant land

As Holy Roman Emperor, Charlemagne sought to contain the insanity of the Byzantine Empire that stood to destabilize Europe. At the same time, factions broke out in Venice, with one trying to break away from the Byzantine Empire to establish a relationship with the Holy Roman Empire and another trying to forge closer relations with the Byzantines.

Charlemagne attempted to claim the Venetian lagoon for the Holy Roman Empire, but failed. He then incorporated the territories of present-day France, Germany, northern Italy, the Low Countries and beyond, linking the Frankish kingdom with Papal lands, in the process forging his own trade routes.

Osnabrück was established in 780, linking the West with key European commercial centers. As a member of the Hanseatic League, Osnabrück became a commercial and defensive confederation of merchant guilds and market towns in Northwestern and Central Europe, pitting the Holy Roman Empire against the Byzantine Empire, the Khazars, and the Venetians for commercial dominance.

By the late 1100s, the Hanseatic League was established to protect the guild's economic interests and diplomatic privileges. The League went on to dominate Baltic maritime trade along the coasts of Northern Europe and then established its own legal system and armies. The two separate and opposing Empires made separate claims to imperial authority and sovereignty, leading to recurring conflict.

Celebrated as the "Father of Europe," Charlemagne united western and central Europe through military force. As Emperor, he spurred a renaissance in cultural and intellectual activity and initiated religious, political, and educational reforms that changed the course of Europe and allowed Christianity to flourish once again. Charlemagne established monasteries and "Palace schools" and instructed priests to learn classical Latin. Under his leadership, scholars produced books on history, poetry, art, music, law, and theology. Christianity and Latin, the language of the church and international communication, spread, helping to unify the European people.

Charlemagne recruited Christian priests to serve as administrators and appointed Jews to positions of finance, medicine, and diplomacy. Meanwhile, the Papacy was reduced to controlling a small portion of land around Rome while it faced constant threats of invasion from the Lombards.

After Charlemagne conquered the Lombards, he added "King of the Lombards" to his title. After giving control of the northern part of Italy to the Pope, Charlemagne created the "Papal States," inspiring Pope Leo III to reward him by crowning Charlemagne "Emperor of the Romans" at Saint Peter's Basilica.

Charlemagne aligned the laws of his kingdom with the laws of God in an effort to administer justice fairly, codify marriage and divorce laws, and establish rights for the people.

Between the late 10th and early 11th century, the Byzantine Empire absorbed parts of Italy and the Mongolian Empire, allowing mercenaries greater movement around its territory.

During the Norman Conquest of Britain in 1066, the Normans claimed the former Byzantine territories in Italy, no doubt opening the door for the gradual infiltration of the Venetians into the British Empire.

Byzantine Emperors recruited Khazars into their government and empires by bribing them with gold. More insanity ensued.

By 1114, the Khazars had established themselves in Constantinople. The Palace of Blachernae was then attacked after Alexios III imprisoned his elder brother, Isaac II Angelos, who had ruled from 1185 to 1195. Alexios then attempted to claim the throne for himself before fleeing to Germany to live with his Catholic relatives. While in Germany, Alexios arranged for leaders of the Crusades to receive money from the Byzantine Empire in exchange for intervention from the Venetian military to help him fortify the city. The Venetians agreed to these terms only to drain the Byzantine treasury, preventing the Empire from paying off it debts, thereby causing the Empire to collapse.

The Crusaders set up a commission to distribute the territories among themselves in the Asia Minor, with Venice claiming territory in the Aegean Sea, or what amounted to half of the Byzantine Empire. The Venetians stripped metal and adornments from churches and sold them on the open market, making the Venetians even richer.

After a Venetian fleet failed to protect the Byzantine Empire from Ottoman Turks, Constantinople fell in 1204.

The Venetians then made off with the four bronze horses from Constantinople and installed them in St. Mark's Basilica in Venice. Adding injury to insult, the Venetians unleashed the "Black Death" in Constantinople, exterminating 90 percent of its population, just in case anyone thought of reclaiming the horses or otherwise retaliating against the Venetians.

In 1245, Pope Innocent VI attempted to launch a Crusade to unite Europe under Christianity with the Pope as the ultimate authority. King Louis IX of France responded with his own Crusade in 1248 to capture Egypt. Meanwhile, Venetian and Genoese merchants were embarking on campaigns to take over Acre, a coastal plain region of the Northern district of Israel situated in a harbor at Haifa Bay on the coast of the Levantine Sea, the easternmost part of the Mediterranean Sea which borders Turkey, Syria, Lebanon, Israel, the Gaza Strip, Egypt, and the Aegean Sea.

The Teutonic Knights, who controlled the tolls at the Acre ports, established the Order of Brothers of the German House of Saint Mary in Jerusalem as a Catholic order for an imperialistic army to assist "Christians" on their pilgrimage to the Holy Land. A Kingdom of Jerusalem was then established by Venetians while they trafficked Southeastern European Christian and Muslims slaves through the area. The Polish Royals claimed that the Knights were expropriating their land and fighting Christians while claiming to defend Christianity.

By 1211, the Knights moved to Transylvania. Prince Charles would later claim Vlad The Impaler as an ancestor. The 15th century ruler became the inspiration for the fictional blood-drinking Count Dracula, who moved from Transylvania to England to spread the curse of the undead and target victims by biting necks with his sharp teeth and drinking blood. Count Dracula was also immortalized in *Sesame Street* as Count von Count, a televised puppet show for children in which The Impaler appears as a friendly Muppet sharing the magic of numbers.

As the son of Vlad Dracul, Vlad the Impaler captured and impaled the envoys of Ottoman Sultan Mehmed II and then led the massacre of tens of thousands of Turks before he retreated to Transylvania. His father belonged to the Order of the Dragon, who were dedicating to fighting "the enemies of Christianity." Yet, these same nobles were actually the enemies of Christianity.

As battles for empire ensued, the Venetians aligned with the Shah of Persia and European royalty, creating a web of interlocking dynasties spanning Europe, the Middle East, and Asia. In the process, Venice became rich in trade through guilds that produced silks, brocades, jewelry, glassware, and other luxury items. At the height of its power, the Venetian Empire was the most powerful economic and military force in Europe.

Their crimes against humanity and attacks against others under the banner of religion continued unabated. In 1489, Rabbi Chemor or Arles wrote to the Grand Sandedrin, the Jewish high court which had a seat in the Venetian-controlled Constantinople, for advice after synagogues were attacked in France. In keeping with Venetian traditions, Chemor responded with what became known as the Constantinople Letter: "As for what you say that the King of France obliges you to become Christians, do it since you cannot do otherwise, but let the law of Moses be kept in your hearts. May your sons be merchants, that little by little they may despoil the Christians of theirs. As for what you say about their making attempts on your lives: make your sons doctors and apothecaries, that they may take away Christian lives. As for what you say of their destroying your synagogues, make your sons canons and clerics that they may destroy their churches. As for many other vexations you complain of, arrange that your sons become advocates and lawyers, and see that they always mix themselves up with the affairs of state, in order that by putting Christians under your yoke, you may dominate the world and be avenged on them. Do not swerve from this order that we give you, because you will find by experience that, humiliated as you are, you will reach the actuality of power." This was the mindset of the barbarian mercenary-merchants. The letter was signed in Constantinople by the Elders of the Jews in 1489 and reprinted by James de Rothschild, in Paris, France in 1889 in the *Revue des Etudes Juives* (*Journal of Jewish Studies*.)

In the name of Judaism, Islam, or Christianity, whatever was most expedient for conquest, the Venetians would assume fictitious identities to win the trust of their hosts countries before subverting them from within. Once their activities were exposed, they would scapegoat others. In keeping with this tradition, the Rothschilds would alternatively identify as Jews or Jesuits sometimes drawing their "moral authority" from their support of Israel – and other times from the Vatican. They labeled anyone who challenged or criticized them as "antisemitic." While the East India Company and Venetians were involved in human trafficking, white Christians who opposed slavery were falsely accused of promoting and condoning this evil institution and then forced to pay reparations, with a bulk of that money going back into the hands of the perpetrators. Through black magic, the Venetians and their agents became skilled at manipulating public perception for the purposes of conquest and fleecing nations. They created illusions and a modality of thinking that others unwittingly embraced.

By the 15th century, the Venetians had created so many enemies that they were warriors non grata everywhere. When the League of Cambria attempted to carve up Venice, the Venetians begged the Ottomans for assistance, but there was none to be had. In the battle of Agnadello, the French defeated the Venetian mercenaries, causing them to lose much of the land they had stolen from others. Many Venetians were driven back to their Lagoon from whence they came. The French then attempted to bankrupt the Venetians to put them out of business for good after a French Ambassador warned French King Louis XII that the Venetians were "traders in human blood, traitors to the Christian faith who have tacitly divided up the world with the Turks, and who are already planning to throw bridgeheads at the Danube, the Rhine, the Seine, and Tagus, and the Ebro, attempting to reduce Europe to a province and to keep it subjugated to their armies."

Others were less charitable. For example, Antonio Contrini, the Patriarch of Aquilea said that the Venetians had reduced its Catholic nuns to prostitutes to serve "the sexual needs of the rich and powerful." Francesco Sforza of Milan said that the Venetians aspired to "conquer Italy and then beyond, thinking to compare themselves to the Romans when their power was at its apex." Niccolò Machiavelli, the author of *The Prince,* a manual for unprincipled, pragmatic leadership, said that the Venetians were "fixed in the intention of creating a monarchy on the Roman model."

The Venetians made no secret of their plans. In 1423, the Doge Tommaso Mocenigo urged Venetians to pursue an aggressive policy of expansion that would make them overlords "of all the gold and of Christendom."

While professing to be Christians, the Venetians refused to serve Christian causes. As a result, they acquired a reputation for dual loyalty. "Prima son Vinizian, poi son Cristian" ("I am a Venetian first, then a Christian,") they would say.

The Venetian Empire was frequently compared to "the whore of Babylon" in *Revelation.* Pope Pius aptly described them as having "the good faith characteristics of barbarians, or after the manner of traders whose nature it is to weigh everything by utility, paying no attention to honor." He then went on to call them "brutish beasts," "aquatic creatures (with) the least intelligence," and "marine monsters" and complained that the Venetians "think only of themselves (and) admire themselves.... They are hypocrites."

On the one hand, Pope Pius said, the Venetians "wish to appear as Christians before the world," but on the other, "they never think of God and, except for the state, which they regard as a deity, they hold nothing sacred, nothing holy....To a Venetian, that is just which is for the good of the state; that is pious which increases the empire.... What the Senate approves is holy even though it is opposed to the *Gospels.* (Venetians) are allowed to do anything that will bring them to supreme power. All laws and rights may be violated for the sake of power....(Their) cause is one with thieves and robbers. No power was ever greater than the Roman Empire, and yet God overthrew it because it was impious. He put in its place the priesthood because it respected divine law.... (They) think (their) republic will last forever. It will not last long. (Its) population so wickedly gathered together will soon be scattered abroad (and) exterminated. A mad state cannot long stand."

During the 1600's, the Venetian fondi (wealth) was transferred north, first to the Bank of Amsterdam and then to later, to the Bank of England. Through the Venetians' relentless quest for empire, aristocrats were assassinated, wealth was plundered, and entire societies were savaged. Wars then broke out throughout the European continent, resulting in the deaths of millions. Peace was temporarily restored and national sovereignty was affirmed with the Treaty of Westphalia, which was signed in 1648 in Münster and Osnabrück which was situated along an important European trading route whose prince-bishop just happened to be the son of a British prince at a time when the British Empire was being infiltrated by Venetian merchants.

Venetian Magic

The Venetians mercenary armies were comprised of nomadic tribes who engaged in occult practices and black magic, which they used to help them defeat enemies. Among the tribes they enlisted were the Mongols who had established trade routes through the

Mongolian Steppes and the Islamic nations, Russia, Europe, and China through a slash and burn policy in which warriors entered foreign lands, butchered communities, plundered treasures, and then moved on before anyone knew what had happened. Their methods were so effective that some Khans had reputedly amassed fortunes valued in the trillions of dollars.

One strategy the Mongols employed involved a type of "magic" in which a small Mongolian army would set fires around a city, leading the people to believe they were surrounded. Terrified, the people would run for cover rather than challenge a small army they easily could have defeated had they mobilized their forces and understood the enemy. In a similar vein, today's corrupt elites try to convince the people that they are powerless to resist an insidious agenda hatched by a handful of elites even though powerlessness is a mindset. There are far more of us (the people) than there are of them (the elites.) By making people feel that the entire system is reinforcing the agenda, the people feel have no choice but to follow it thereby succumbing to a type of Mongolian "magic." If the people understood their strength in numbers, they could easily resist the agenda and reclaim their power.

Another Mongolian tactic involved dividing up their army, sending some of their troops behind the enemy, and coordinating attacks with messengers traveling at high speed between the front and the back. While the front half attacked, the enemy would turn around to flee only to be slaughtered by the Mongols in the back. Another tactic involved pretending to surrender in battle. As their Mongols retreated, their enemy would run after them in disorganized chaos. The Mongols would then turn around and destroy their pursuers.

The Mongols even plundered gold and slayed the noble Chinese Song dynasty, whose patronage of the sciences had led to great technological discoveries. The Mongols then set up a base in Beijing for the Venetians, establishing a small class of rulers and large class of slaves, with taxes imposed upon the slaves to generate passive income for the elites through legalized theft while the elites lived tax-free.

The Tibetan monks also kept occult secrets that helped the Venetians prevail in war. While the Dalai Lama presents himself as a deeply religious man, Tibetan practices are reputedly steeped in an anti-human death cult, as can be seen in Tibetan art, which depicts images of skulls, demon possession, and terror.

The Venetians acquired access to Tibet after Genghis Khan, the Supreme Khan of the Mongolian tribes, slashed and burned his way through China in the 13th century while serving in Venetian mercenary armies.

The nomadic mercenary hordes practiced a religion called Bon-po, or some variation of this, which was based upon animism or black magic that originated from Persia. The occult shamans were convinced that through black magic, they could walk with the Gods, ascend to the heavens, and descend into hell, initiating people into death and rebirth, not through spiritual renewal but a form of reincarnation that would somehow allow them to cheat death while inflicting death upon others. As "enlightened" beings, they believed they possessed divine souls that elevated them above ordinary mortals.

A pre-Buddhist spiritual and religious culture of Tibet, Bon involved evoking ecstasy through ritual magic to manipulate energy (Bon-po). To acquire power and good fortune, they dabbled in the occult and performed human and animal sacrifices which they believed invoked demons and demonic armies who could serve them. Pedophilia was also an accepted practice among the Tibetan monks. Boys recruited to the monkhood were expected to be sexually pleasing to the monks and to bring them good fortune on penalty of death.

Convinced that commercialism and modernization had destroyed the planet, the Tibetan monks sought to deindustrialize earth to limit human consumption to that required for feeding and caring for farm animals before slaughter while they enjoyed luxuries and privileges denied everyone else, befitting their status as Gods. The mentality they held is similar to that espoused by today's ruling elites. Exterminating people through war helped them expand their "living space" and enjoy a higher standard of living, with wealth acquired from the fallen.

The Tibetan "bon-po" is represented by the Nazi symbol, which is not surprising given that the Nazis traveled to Tibet to acquire the forbidden, occult knowledge of the monks. In Tibetan language, Yungdrung Bon translates into the Swastika to represent an unchangeable, indestructible, Buddha-like state of mind, the light of existence.

As Gnostics, Tibetan priests believe that man is separate from spirit. This is also seen in Aryanism, or unity through nobility which holds the notion that if Jesus could rise to the level of God and be worshiped, then so could they. Rather than worship God, they aspired to live as Gods through the powers of black magic. It is not surprising, then, that Ogadai Khan (the son of Genghis Khan) rejected Pope Innocent IV's attempts to convert the Mongols to Christianity on grounds that "What do you mean we should become Christians? I am the instrument of your God.... We have destroyed the whole earth from the East and the West in the power of God." Mangu Khan remarked that "In heaven there is but one eternal God. On earth, there is but one Lord Genghis Khan, the son of God."

For slight offenses, the Mongols plucked out eyes and lopped off noses and appendages. Dismembered body parts were fed to the dogs. Some monks, who had acquired a taste for human blood, descended to cannibalism. Sexual promiscuity was encouraged and condoned and human skulls and bones acquired through human sacrifices were used as utensils and musical instruments.

The Mongols believed that non-human entities contained souls and that they could communicate with demons. As followers of Tengrism, they believed they had a mandate from Tengri, the ruler of Heaven, to rule the world. At the same time, they were "tolerant" of other religions due to their nomadic lifestyles, accounting for their desire to blend all religions into one universal faith. While shunning religion, they built houses of worship for Buddhism, Islam, Christianity, and Taoism and provided financial support for Buddhist monasteries, Confucian scholarship, Islamic mosques, and Christian churches.

III.
Victoria's Secret

The French and American Revolutions were inspired by the principles of the Venetian "rational Enlightenment," which metastasized like a cancer throughout Europe. The murderous, violent tactics of the revolutionaries were specifically geared at upsetting the existing order so that the would-be conquerors could seize the assets and power from those who had it and claim it for themselves, not through divine providence, bloodline, or initiation, but through the barrel of a gun. If Christianity and Judaism inspired reverential devotion to God, the rationalists rejected God altogether while arguing that inalienable rights granted by God could be secured through revolution.

In order for them to become the undisputed tyrants of a Roman Empire that would extend throughout the world, the Venetians would need to erase the "divine rite to rule" and install themselves in power through violence and deception. "You are of your father, the devil," Jesus told those who worshiped the false God. "He was a murderer from the beginning and does not stand in truth because there is no truth in him. Whenever he speaks a lie, he speaks from his own nature for he is a liar and the father of lies." (*John14:17*). Ironically, the followers of the rational Enlightenment were decidedly lacking in wisdom and were often self-defeating. In the eyes of others, they often seemed insane.

Ayn Rand's objectivism epitomized this attitude brilliantly – one of rugged individualism in pursuit of power and profit in which every choice and decision is based upon a rational cost-benefit analysis, providing the justification for the moral lapses of corporations in pursuit of profits. On the more extreme side, murder and revolution can be justified as a rational basis to acquire more wealth and power even if one must to appeal to lofty principles to rally unsuspecting people to the cause. Rand encouraged others to pursue their self-interest while withholding assistance to those in need. While the Rothschilds subsidized her books, including *The Fountainhead* and *Atlas Shrugged,* she ended her life living on welfare, without the kindness of strangers. It was almost as if by denying humanity, these people became less than human themselves.

Among the new generation of Enlightened despots was Russian Empress Catherine the Great. Born in 1729 as an impoverished princess from Germany, Catherine married the Grand Duke Peter of Holstein. The couple was trained to "modernize" Russia – that is, to chip away at the status quo so the shadow elite could seize control of the country and its resources. Once installed in power, the couple promoted the principles of the Venetian Enlightenment. As "sophisticated" and "modern" people, they flouted moral standards, laws, and convention.

Libertinism proved to be their undoing. Catherine quickly grew tired of her drunken, doltish husband who missed his own coronation. She also lost respect for him after he dissolved the Russian Empire and surrendering land in Britain's ally, Prussia, without a fight.

While the Rothschilds stoked revolution in France, Catherine corresponded with leading philosophers of the French Enlightenment, including Voltaire and Diderot. Voltaire was so impressed with Catherine's Enlightened despotism that he called her the "star of the North." Intoxicated with power and tired of her husband's antics, Catherine forced Peter's abdicated and ordered his assassination, effectively, committing regicide.

As sole ruler, Catherine II oversaw the expansion of the Russian Empire through military conquests. Her endless virtue signaling cloaked brazen power grabs. She colonized Alaska, which was later sold to the United States, enabling Rothschild interests to assume controlling interests over the Eskimos and their oil. Later, when Henry Kissinger became Secretary of State, the United States would be prevented from tapping that oil, to reduce America's energy independence and make the United States dependent upon foreign oil, providing a pretext for war and resources to fuel the Rothschild war machine.

As an Enlightened despot, Catherine publicly expressed

sympathy for the plight of serfs while refusing to improve their general welfare. She sponsored schools and libraries only to stifle intellectual discovery and debate by standardizing education. As a patron of the arts, she amassed one of the largest art collections in the world through the spoils of war. Throughout her reign, Catherine conferred wealth and prestige upon loyalists. While the Rothschilds were shoring up Russia's assets for London's banking district, Catherine had an affair with a Polish secretary to a British envoy in Russia. Having embraced Enlightened despotism with flourish, she died in an act of bestiality with a stallion whose supporting harness snapped at an inopportune time, crushing her instantly.

Backstabbing Bankers

A Roman statesman once said that "a nation can survive its fools and even the ambitious, but it cannot survive treason from within – for the traitor appears not a traitor. He speaks in the accents familiar to his victims, and he appeals to the baseness that lies deep in the hearts of all men. He rots the soul of a nation. He works secretly and unknown in the night to undermine the pillars of a city. He infects the body politic so that it can no longer resist." Such were the tactics of the scheming Venetians whose cancerous ways would infect the entire world.

The Venetians transformed the European continent into a bloodbath through the Ottoman Wars (1265-1453) and the Hundred Years War (1337-1453). They then challenged the Ottoman Empire again in the 16th century, with the Venetians forming an alliance with the Holy League, including the Pope, Jesuits, and the Republic of Genoa – the Republic of Venice's chief maritime rival. Once the Byzantine Empire collapsed in 1453, the Venetians pursued "rational Enlightenment," a political strategy that enabled them to erode the authority of Monarchs and establish constitutional, elective governments.

The Holy Roman Empire was established as an elective

monarchy, with its Monarchs and prince electors selected through an electoral college based in Frankfurt. The prince electors then selected the Emperor, not unlike the American electoral college which ultimately selects the President of the United States. From 1440 to 1740, a member of the Habsburg dynasty was always Emperor, making this position effectively hereditary.

The Holy Roman Empire stretched across northern Italy and towards the Papal States, opening the doors for Venetian infiltration into the Habsburg dynasty through the provinces of Lombardy and Venice. The Habsburgs had attempted to arrange a marriage between the Protestant Queen Elizabeth I and and Catholic Holy Roman Emperor Charles V (Archduke Charles of Austria), but the Queen rejected this proposal in the interests of preserving the British Monarchy as head of the Church of England.

The origins of the Rothschild family are a bit of a mystery. Suffice to say, the dynasty's patriarch was able to exploit the strategies, tactics, and networks of the Venetians to establish one of the most powerful dynasties in the world. Mayer Amschel Rothschild (1744-1812) founded the House of Rothschild in Frankfurt am Main, an imperial city within the Holy Roman Empire.

The Rothschild patriarch set up his coin counting shop in Frankfurt, which was an important center for commercial and political power. While his last name was "Bauer," Rothschild decided to claim the name of his 16th century ancestors whose house was emblazoned with the name "zum roten shild," meaning "to the red sign." The symbol of the red cross represents the Knights Templar, who had guided Pilgrims on their journeys to Jerusalem. The red hexagram on Rothschild's door translates geometrically and numerically into the number 666 (Satan) to signify the Seal of Solomon, which also encompasses the yin-and-yang symbol – that is, the balancing of good and evil for Luciferians which can be seen on the Tibetan flag.

Mayer Amschel Rothschild began his career as an apprentice at the Hanover-based Oppenheimer Bank. Through contacts and opportunities acquired through this bank, Rothschild was able to become a financial advisor to the British Monarchy at a time when

King George III was an elector of Brunswick-Lüneburg (Hanover) in the Holy Roman Empire. While working in Hanover, Rothschild was introduced to Prince William IX of Hesse through General Von Estorff, effectively launching the banker's career. He then became financial advisor to the Prince.

A financial genius who had inherited one of the largest fortunes in Europe, William imparted his financial knowledge upon Rothschild who used his connections with the Prince to provide Hessian mercenaries to the British King to put down Venetian-inspired skirmishes on the North American continent. The Hessians were trained in Britain and bankrolled by Rothschilds, a feat made possible through access he had acquired through the East India Company. By financing skirmishes between the British Monarchy and the North American colonies, Rothschild was able to create the conditions for war which then allowed him to finance both sides of the American Revolution.

While remaining highly secretive about his own affairs, he relied heavily upon Venetian spy networks so that gain the strategic advantage in all matters of concern to him. As luck would have it, Frankfurt was the headquarters for the postal service that Holy Roman Emperor Maximilian I established in 1516, connecting Vienna, Brussels, and Central Europe. Through this postal service, Rothschild and his agents were able to intercept mail to acquire knowledge on troop movements, government activities, and Monarch correspondence. This, in turn, provided the dynasty valuable intelligence which they used to topple governments and win wars that they bankrolled, directed, and managed.

The Rothschilds had succeeded in driving King George III mad so that he would be easier to control. King George III's son, William IV, was next in line for the throne. In an effort to make a name for himself, William IV joined the Royal Navy. While fighting in the American Revolution, William attempted to kidnap Gen. George Washington. Since the Venetians had spies in both camps, they were able to tip off the future President to the young heir's schemes and derail his plans.

According to the historian Lord David Cecil: "William IV

was a classic example of a man not up to this job. As a Prince, he had been merely harmless and comical – a bustling, chattering buffoon of a sailor, with a head shaped like a pineapple and a large troops of illegitimate children. As a King, he made more a disturbing impression. On the throne of England, a buffoon is no laughing matter. As King, he set up a democratic monarch suitable to the new democratic age. He was so ungrounded and frightened that he turned into a panicky reactionary who smelt bloody revolution in every breath. His ministers did not take him seriously although he found that being King was not the pleasure he had hoped it was going to be, with the result that the jolly old buffoon became a surly touchy bewildered old buffoon who sought to compensate for a sense of impotence by bombarding his ministers with reams of futile complaining and inept advice." William IV was convinced that England was on "a slipper slope to an atheistic republic" – and not without cause.

When Britain declared war on France in 1793, William IV expected a command befitting a future King, but was not even given a ship. After delivering a speech against war, he fell down a flight of stairs while drunk and broke his arm. Some say he was pushed. While the Rothschilds financed Royals, financing was withheld from William IV, preventing him from being able to support himself or find a suitable Royal spouse. His efforts at gainful employment were frustrated at every turn. In order to survive, he courted wealthy actresses and courtesans until he found one who would cohabit with him. Together they produced 10 illegitimate children, but no viable heirs.

The bloodline was still intact through King George III's other son, Ernest Augustus who sired Prince George of Cumberland.

Since William produced no heirs, his niece, Princess Victoria was next in line to the throne. Before her coronation, Victoria was subjected to "continuous turmoil of intrigue and conflict," Lord Cecil wrote. "Victoria had never been treated by the English Royal family with the respect due to her." And why would she be after the Royal Family was forced to sell breeding rights to the Rothschild dynasty who would breed their disgusting selves into the Monarchy and into Royal families throughout Europe?

Surrounded by personal and political advisors, Victoria took actions that preserved the sacred Royal blood line that the Rothschilds were attempting to extinguish forever. Among her advisors were the Lord Melbourne, who served as British Prime Minister from 1835 to 1841 and was Victoria's close friend and political adviser; and the Duke of Wellington whom Victoria considered a "father figure." Appreciating that the very legitimacy of the Monarchy was at stake, Victoria secretly married Prince George of Cumberland. Together they produced a legitimate heir who retained the sacred bloodline. The heir was quietly shuffled off to Portugal so that he would remain safe and beyond the reach of the murderous revolutionaries;

Victoria then married her consort, Prince Albert, committing bigamy. By this point, the Rothschilds had bought, conned, and finagled their way into the Royal bloodline. As a result, Victoria was forced to give birth to a succession of illegitimate children, all of whom were Rothschild bastards, a feat she described as "the shadow side of marriage." As she explained to one of her daughters in 1858: "What you say of the pride of giving life to an immortal soul is very fine, but I own I cannot enter into that; I think much more of our being like a cow or a dog at such moments; when our poor nature becomes so very animal and unecstatic."

By her coronations, revolutionary fervor was consuming Britain as the Rothschilds sought to usurp the divine right to rule and establish a constitutional monarchy – that is, a Royal family reigned in by a representative government the dynasty and its agents controlled. "Revolutions are always bad for the country, and the cause of untold misery to the people," Victoria lamented. Instead she preferred "obedience to the laws and to a higher Power, divinely instituted for the good of the people, not the Sovereign, who has equally duties and obligations."

With the Rothschilds secretly controlling the throne, revolution raged through Britain. "At the beginning of 1830," Lord Cecil wrote, "the movement for parliamentary reform flared up with new and extraordinary fury all over England. As the year advanced so did the cause. George IV's death removed a powerful obstacle to reform. While in Paris, the bloodless revolution of July showed timid reformers that drastic change could be accomplished without catastrophe. By the end of the summer, feeling in the country was stirred to a pitch of excitement unknown. In the houses of the great and the clubs of St. James (whose members consisted of merchants of the East India Company) an atmosphere as before a thunder storm tense with ominous expectancy hung heavy over the political scene. Everybody felt that something tremendous was going to happen; nobody quite knew what."

The game plan in play was to sweep away the old guard, those who held wealth and power, and claim it for a shadowy subversive group led by Rothschild. As Lord David Cecil wrote in *Melbourne*: "The great Whig country houses of the 18th and 19th centuries was a unique product of English civilization. It was before all things a governing class. At a time when economic power was concentrated in the landed interests, the Whigs were among the greatest land owners. Their party was in power for the greatest part of the 18th century. During this period, they held large portion of seats in the House of Commons. The man of sense and taste was he whose every activity was regulated in the light of a trained judgment and the experience of the wise in his own and former ages. From his earliest years, the Whig nobleman was subjected to a careful education. He was grounded in the classics first by a tutor, then at Eton, then at University. After this he went abroad for two years grand tour to learn French and good manners in the best of society of the Continent. In everything they paid strict attention to form. Their ideal was the Renaissance ideal of the whole man whose aspiration it is to make the most of every advantage, intellectual and sensual that life has to offer. By the iron laws which condition the social structure of man's existence, it could last only as long as it maintained an economic preponderance. With the coming of the industrial revolution, this predominance began to pass from the landlords to the other ranks of the community. Already by the close of the century, go ahead manufacturers in the north were talking of

Parliamentary reform. In the upper rooms of obscure London alleys, working men met together to clamour for liberty, equality, and fraternity. Within forty years of its zenith, the Whig world was complete swept away." The reformers were a "heterogeneous body of radical democrats, political theorists and dissenters and the bulk of the manufacturers all those believed in reform and liked it," Lord Cecil said.

As Prime Minister, the Eton-educated Duke of Wellington resisted Rothschild's pressure for constitutional reform to the detriment of his political career. The Duke's reputation was that of "servant of the Monarch and the people." When radicals threatened to blackmail him in order to sway his opinion, he said, "publish and be damned." As the Iron Duke, he was known for his discipline, simplicity and lack of ego. " I am but a man," he said. As Prime Minister he put down the Chartist movement without violence.

For his part, Melbourne rejected parliamentary reform on grounds that it would lead to the "total destruction of the freedom of speech (and) inevitably fail to produce all of the benefits hoped for from it." For all his resistance, Melbourne appreciated that the manufacturers and their agents had the upper hand, and so he gently resisted revolutionary demands while quietly accommodating them.

Melbourne's Foreign Secretary was Lord Palmerston who mentored Karl Marx, Giuseppe Mazzini, among other revolutionaries. Describing the zeitgeist of the times, Lord Cecil wrote: "The new spirit showed itself in the world of politics. Signs were visible on every side that the struggle between the old aristocratic landed regime and the new individualistic democratic forces could not be delayed much longer. The restless discontent of those classes who were shut out from political power began to make itself felt, seeping up from the world of revolutionary agitators to infuse itself into the respectable middle and professional classes. Everywhere the cry was reform; law reform, educational reform, fiscal reform of the laws against nonconformists and Roman Catholics. Parliamentary reform was the crucial issue. For, by destroying the aristocracy's monopoly on the seats in the House of Commons, it wrestled from it at one stroke the control of government. With it the men of the new age would be in a position to impose any other change they wanted; without it they could move only permission of their opponents."

At the time, spies and agent provocateurs attempted to discover the ringleaders of the revolts, but Melbourne prevented discovery, presumably as he had the ear of Queen Victoria and knew that the Rothschilds controlled the throne from the shadows. To reveal the ringleaders would have been professional suicide. "I am sure you must feel that in our anxiety to discover the perpetrators of these most dangerous and atrocious acts, we should run as little risk as possible in involving innocent persons in accusations and still less of adopting measures which may encourage the seduction of persons now innocent into the commission of crime," Melbourne said.

At the time, there were clear indications of organized revolution through unions. "The only function (of unions) was to maintain law and order while reform was going through," Lord Cecil wrote. Overnight unions had sprung up all over Britain whose aims were "openly revolutionary (with) sinister rumors of arms practice after dark." Without naming the organizers, Melbourne said, "people who talk much of railroads and bridges are generally liberals." At the time, the Rothschilds were financing railroads and bridges in Britain and around Europe.

With the Rothschilds and their Venetian allies fomenting revolution, Parliament demanded power to make peers – that is, to install representatives who checked the power of the Monarch and answered to the Rothschilds while advancing the interests of the rising class of industrialists driven by Rothschild. "Parliament in its reformed state is made up of manufacturers, nonconformists, and other dingy and unpredictable persons," Lord Cecil wrote. "Radicals looked at reform of Parliament as a necessary step toward general reform – reform of the church, reform of the local government, reform of Ireland, reform of the House of Lords."

During the reform period, violent marauding mobs stormed through towns, demanding "bread or blood."

"Hungry workers of the industrial towns were forming

themselves into sinister communal organizations called trade unions who spent their nights secretly drilling and who had the purpose of ousting their employers from the rightful command of their labor," Lord Cecil wrote. "Strikes and riots broke out in which one employer was actually murdered. What made the situation especially alarming was that outside London there was as yet no regular police force and that the army which alone filled its place was a handful of men. To the propertied class, it seemed as if the very foundations of civilized life were crumbling beneath their feet. A wave of panic swept over them."

While working at the Home Office, Melbourne received "fantastic alarmist tales of a deep laid Jesuit plot," including a plot to overthrow the Constitution, leading Melbourne to take action to restore order. "Order was restored within months," Lord Cecil wrote. "To force nothing but force can be successfully opposed," Melbourne said. "It is evident that all legislation is impotent and ridiculous unless the public peace can be preserved and the liberty and property of individuals saved from outrage and invasion."

At the time, Britain was "teetering on the edge of bloodstained chaos," Lord Cecil wrote. "Responsible people woke every morning to hear of mobs burning down houses and robbing harmless citizens, without anyone being able to stop them. What made these events more ominous was that the men who composed the mobs were no worse off than they had often been during recent years yet never before had they broken out in this sinister fashion. It looked as if these disturbances must be deliberately provoked by some revolutionary plot."

Rothschild money had spurred the industrial revolution within England. With money, came a demand for power. "The industrial revolution by turning England from an agricultural to a manufacturing country began to disturb that balance which must exist in any society between political and economic power," Lord Cecil wrote. "No longer were the land and its aristocratic owners the sole masters of the country's wealth. This position was shared by a new and rising class, part manufacturers, part workmen, who now demanded a voice in the government of the nation proportionate to their economic influence. Nonconformists, free traders, and of humble birth, they noted with irritation that the country was run in the interests of protectionists, Anglicans, and Lords. They clamoured for legal reform, fiscal reform, religious emancipation. Above all they asked for that parliamentary reform which by destroying the aristocratic monopoly of seats would readjust the balance of government in their favor. And they invoked all manner of novel and alarming doctrines – equality; the rights of man, the principles of unity – to give moral justification for their claims. How far and in what manner these claims might be granted, by what means existing institutions could be modified in harmony with the new balance of power, were to be the problems that occupied the next four years of English history."

Reflecting the hidden hand of the secret occult Venetian infiltration, Lord Cecil wrote: "In England – unions hovered around a murky atmosphere of violence and conspiracy; admission to them was accompanied by all sorts of melodramatic initiation ceremonies involving skulls and oaths of silence and names signed in human blood." They also took direct aim at the church: "The church of England was entering upon one of the most strenuous and turmoiled phases of its history. Like other traditional English institutions it had woken from the placid summer afternoon slumber of the 18th century to find itself in a strange and disturbing world. The rise of liberalism political and intellectual appeared to be threatening its very existence. On every side were menacing cries of atheist, radicals, now demanding its disestablishment, not questioning the very foundation of the Christian faith."

At the same time England was moving closer to the Vatican which sought to replace the divine right to rule with Vatican appointments. Rothschild was the shadow force behind the Vatican too. "Towards the church of Rome (the Prime Minister's) manner was respectable," Lord Cecil wrote. "No doubt it was superstitious and tyrannical, and (the Prime Minister) was extremely glad that England was not under its sway, but the church of Rome was an ancient and venerable institution that appealed to his historic sense and with which he thought it wise the English government should be on good terms. He regretted that Protestant bigotry made it impossible for him to get an Ambassador to the Vatican. He made efforts to get into good unofficial relations there, " but was not entirely successful.

Demanding an overturn of a political structure that did not automatically capitulate, revolutionaries proceeded to set Parliament on fire. Melbourne "watched the huge conflagration as it reflected itself in the dark waters of the Thames," Lord Cecil wrote. "His heart was filled with strange and mournful emotions. The spectacle was symbolic. The England he had always known was being destroyed before his eyes."

Mayer Amschel Rothschild sired five sons, who were each assigned a country in which to establish a banking business as part of a ground operation for world conquest. One son, Nathan, founded N.M. Rothschild & Sons, in London at 2 New Court at St. Swithin's Lane near the Bank of England and the London Stock Exchange. The London branch of the Rothschild business extended loans to France, Russia -- and South America, where the Rothschilds were busy separating European Monarchs from their colonies and establishing puppet governments. Nathan arrived in England in 1798 and then moved to 107 Piccadilly in 1825. Other Rothschild relatives followed suit, inspiring neighbors to nickname Green Park "Rothschild Row," a street situated next to Buckingham Palace. The Rothschild's London branch was nestled within in City of Westminster, the heart of the British government. Amschel Mayer Rothschild continued his father's legacy in Frankfurt while Jacob Rothschild set up shop in Paris; Solomon Rothschild was dispatched to Vienna; and Calman Rothschild established a branch in Naples, an important center of Venetian Enlightenment and humanism. While the Rothschilds assumed the role of trusted government advisors, financiers, and business executives, they were quietly plotting the overthrow of governments worldwide with a view to installing themselves as world dictators presiding over a socialist technocracy in which they ruled as Gods over everyone else.

Napoleon Complex

The Rothschild patriarch owed his fortune to Prince William IX of Hesse, the East India Company, and the American Revolution. With his newfound wealth, Rothschild directed French Emperor Napoleon Bonaparte to attack the Holy Roman Empire and Great Britain, with Rothschild providing the financing to help them fight Napoleon whom he had also bankrolled. While Napoleon was attempting to seize the assets of aristocrats in the Holy Roman Empire, William IX enlisted Rothschild to hide his wealth from Napoleon. Rothschild turned around and gave the money to his son, Nathan Rothschild, in London. Nathan used the prince's wealth to finance British movements throughout Portugal and Spain in an effort to topple governments there.

As Napoleon advanced on the Holy Roman Empire, William IX, was exiled, and his electorate was annexed by the Kingdom of Westphalia which was subsequently managed by Jérôme Bonaparte, Napoleon's brother who was bankrolled by Rothschild.

After Napoleon purged the elected princes from the Holy Roman Empire, the French Emperor appointed Karl von Dalberg, a Rothschild agent, to rule the new Confederation of the Rhine, where Frankfurt was located, ensuring Rothschild would be shielded from retaliation inspired by his betrayal.

Giving hint to the traitors within the British Empire, Napoleon was trained at British military schools before he threatened to invade England as French Emperor. Napoleon's grandfather was linked to a French Jacobite army led by Charles Edward Stuart who disembarked on the coast of Scotland, falsely claiming to be the rightful heir to the Scottish throne. Napoleon's last name of "Bone Parte" is a French derivative of "Bone Party," a veiled reference to the secret Babylonian death cult. Napoleon Bonaparte (Napoleon I) was born in Corsica, an island in the Mediterranean Sea that the Habsburg dynasty used to transmit communications and intelligence collected from Italy, Spain, and the Holy Roman Empire. Charlemagne had claimed the island for the

Holy Roman Empire only to relinquish it later to the Venetian-controlled Byzantine Empire after a military invasion. The island was then transferred to the Republic of Genoa, which formed a union with Great Britain after the French Revolution. Once the union was established, Napoleon's grandfather staged a failed coup against the Scottish Monarchy.

While Napoleon burned through Europe, Venice agreed to remain neutral "Be neutral, but see that your neutrality be indeed sincere and perfect," Napoleon told the Venetians. "If any insurrection occurs in my rear to cut off my communications in the event of my marching on Germany---if any movement whatever betray the disposition of your Senate to aid the enemies of France, be sure that vengeance will follow---from that hour the independence of Venice has ceased to be."

After Venice affirmed its neutrality, Napoleon said, "The only course to be taken is to destroy this ferocious and sanguinary government – and erase the Venetian name from the face of the earth." The French Emperor went so far as to accuse the Venetians of having "treacherously shed French blood" and "murdered my children."

Even though Venice was the source of the revolutionary spirit spreading throughout Europe, Napoleon remarked that Venice's "whole territory (was) imbued with revolutionary principles. One single word from me will excite a blaze of insurrection through all your provinces. Ally yourself with France, make a few modifications in your government, such as are indispensable for the welfare of the people, and we will pacify public opinion and will sustain your authority." Having invented and executed these strategies over centuries, the Venetians respectfully rebuffed Napoleon.

Through the international Venetian spy networks, Napoleon heard that the Venetian Doge (chief magistrate ruler) had raised taxes and that the Venetians could unleash an army of 50,000 men, comprised of fierce and semi-barbarous mercenaries, to contain him.

In 1797, Napoleon invaded Venice and seized the horses

that the Venetians had stolen from Constantinople. Venice then surrendered territory, war ships, gold, and art, including the celebrated picture of St. Jerome from the Duke of Parma's gallery, reflecting oligarch upon oligarch plunder. When the Duke attempted to retrieve the picture Napoleon had stolen by bribing him to return it, Napoleon replied: "The sum which (you) offer us will soon be spent, but the possession of such a masterpiece at Paris will adorn the capital for ages and give birth to similar exertions of genius."

In keeping with the principles of the rational Enlightenment, Napoleon closed Venetian churches and monasteries and then claimed Venice for France, ending the Venetian Republic. The Doge was forced to abdicate in 1797.

Venice was then used as a bargaining chip for the Rothschilds who had dislodged aristocrats and Monarchs through revolutions and coups and implanted puppet governments in their place. Austria swapped Lombardy for Venice and then installed its own people into the Venetian government. The Rothschilds controlled Austria through finance. Concluding that the Venetian rulers were privileged, but uneducated and undisciplined warriors who owed their position to nepotism, inheritance, and plunder, the Austrians would not allow the Venetians to assume positions of responsibility within the new government. Napoleon then dismantled the Austrian Empire and established obedient puppet governments. Once Napoleon was exiled in 1815, the Rothschilds "rescued" the four horses and returned them to St. Mark's Basilica in Venice, with a wink and a nod.

While Napoleon was attempting to conquer Europe and install himself as dictator, other revolutionaries came to the fore to promote revolution which defended religious beliefs, including, for example, Giuseppe Mazzini, an Italian politician, journalist, and activist who promoted the unification of Italy and spearheaded the Italian revolutionary movement. In the nineteenth century, Britain's Lord Palmerston, a liberal British foreign secretary who later became prime minister, groomed Mazzini to foment revolution. One of Palmerston's principal operatives, David Urquhart, was Karl Marx's handler.

Born is Genoa during the First French Empire, Mazzini was indoctrinated in the revolutionary spirit and given publicity for his ideas. Mazzini's father taught Jacobin philosophy at a university. With generous private funding, Mazzini organized Young Italy, a secret society promoting Italian unification as "one free independent republican nation."

Not content to just "liberate" Italy, Mazzini offered pseudo-Christian arguments to advance Rothschild's vision for a federated Europe based upon the principles of the Venetian rational Enlightenment. To this end, Mazzini promoted a federal assembly to establish national assemblies. He then organized Young Germany, Young Poland, Young Switzerland, Young Turks, and other Young European Movements. The European Movement that Prime Minister Winston Churchill would later establish after World War II to advance Rothschild's vision for a federal European state, was based upon this model.

Mazzini attempted to enlist Christians in the revolutionary movement by characterizing Karl Marx as "a destructive spirit whose heart was filled with hatred rather than love of mankind." Marx had a few choice words for him in return.

The secret elite financed and supported all sides of a movement to control the process and outcome. Marx, he said, advocated "communist egalitarianism" while declaring himself "the absolute ruler of his party." At the same time, Mazzini said, Marx "gives orders and tolerates no opposition." A deist who believed in "divine providence," Mazzini professed his Christian faith while denouncing rationalism and atheism. Even though he was an internationalist, he claimed that his patriotism was born out of a love for Italy.

Breaking the Bank

The Rothschilds sought nothing short of world conquest. To this end, they directed Napoleon to wage war against Britain whose military was led by the Duke of Wellington. Part of the Rothschild strategy involved crushing Britain's industry through blockades. Once the companies experienced financial distress, Nathan Rothschild offered to bail them out. "When I settled in London, the East India Company had eight hundred pounds worth of gold to sell," Nathan Rothschild said in *Romance of the Rothschilds*. "I went to the sale and bought it all. I knew the Duke of Wellington (who was leading the troops for Britain against Napoleon) must have it. I had bought a great many of his bills at a discount. The (British) Government sent for me and said they must have it. When they got it, they did not know how to get it to Portugal. I undertook all that and sent it through France. It was the best business that I have ever done."

While Napoleon was implementing the Continental System to blockade Britain, new manufacturing was stimulated in France. At the same time, other regions dependent upon overseas commerce were financially devastated. Napoleon's fleet became overstretched as it attempted to enforce the blockade against the British. As a result, Napoleon was unable to wage a successful campaign against Russia, inspiring the Russian composer Pyotr Illyich Tchaikovsky to write the *Overture of 1812*, a 15 minute musical replete with a volley of cannon fire marking Napoleons' defeat. In 1817, the Rothschilds purchased the rights to the *Overture*.

In response to Napoleon's blockage, Britain formed a counter-blockade. The British then kidnapped American sailors and forced them to serve in the British Navy to beef up their manpower. The big showdown between the British and French took place at the Battle of Waterloo. While the Rothschilds had financed Napoleon's campaign against Britain, they boasted in their promotional materials that they had "won the contract" to fund the Duke of Wellington's final campaign against Napoleon in the Battle of Waterloo in 1815.

Napoleon first appeared to be winning. After the Prussians sent reinforcements, the tide turned toward Wellington. Nathan Rothschild then received news by way of a carrier pigeon that Napoleon had lost the war. He sought to capitalize by selling all of his stock in the London stock market at its peak. Others witnessing what he was doing followed suit, thinking Britain had lost to Napoleon. As a result, the stock market crashed. Rothschild then rushed in and bought all the stock at rock bottom prices, ensuring he had a controlling interest in British companies and was in complete control of the British economy. A new Bank of England was then established under Rothschild's control. Once knowledge of Napoleon's defeat spread, the stock market soared, making Nathan Rothschild the wealthiest man in Britain. That year, Nathan Mayer Rothschild became "Nathan Mayer Baron de Rothschild."

After losing money in the market, the British Royal Family needed to be bailed out. Rothschild agreed to do so in exchange for the right to breed into the Royal bloodline, usurping the divine rite to rule. As a result, he was able to establish a Royal Rothschild bloodline. This allowed the dynasty to control the British Monarchy through illegitimate heirs and to breed itself into Royal families and governments throughout Europe, thus beginning the secret Rothschild breeding program which enabled the dynasty to infiltrate, corrupt, and compromise governments around the world with few people being aware of the infiltration.

Having generated debt through war, the French took out loans through government bonds organized by the Duke of Wellington from two opposing banks, Ouvard in France and the Barings Brothers in London. In October of 1818, Rothschild agents then began buying French government bonds, dramatically increasing their value. In the ensuing months, these bonds were dumped in the open market, creating a financial panic that destroyed their value. As a result, the banks no longer had surety for their loans. The Rothschilds then had complete control over France's economy.

Moses Montefiore and Nathan Mayer Rothschild also loaned the British Treasury £3,200,000 for debt owed to the privately operated Bank of England, which was operated by Nathan Rothschild. The debt was serviced in exchange for granting the Rothschilds exclusive trading privileges with all countries of the Indian and Pacific Oceans between Cape Horn and Cape Good

Hope for newly chartered joint stock corporations modeled after the East India Company. These companies eventually formed the basis for the multinationals that the Rothschilds and their networks would control through interlocking boards of directors.

Their corporate executives fleeced public treasuries and pension funds, bribed and corrupted public officials, and directed governments to give them preferential treatment and advantages over the national interest and the interests of citizens. Governments were used as weapons to eliminate competition and provide unlimited funding for their enterprises. Increasingly, the corrupt shadow elite, which centered around Rothschild, used its advantages to strip nations, businesses, and people of their wealth with a view towards owning the world and relegating others to the status of slaves to serve them. Werner Sombart wrote that from 1820 onward, "there was only one power in Europe and that was Rothschild."

Nathan's son, Lionel Rothschild, built 148 Piccadilly next to Number 1 London, or the Apsley House, the townhouse of the Duke of Wellington, who had amassed an incredible art collection while bankrolled by the Rothschilds. Much of the art had been seized by Napoleon during his march through Europe and then "rescued" by the Rothschilds who gave it to Wellington to showcase in his house for safekeeping. The Duke's house contained over 3,000 fine paintings, sculptures, and works of art fashioned in silver, porcelain, batons, swords and seized from fallen Emperors, Tsars and Kings.

The Duke of Wellington's new Georgian home acquired paintings from the Spanish royal collections, including Velásquez, Murillo, Rubens, Goya, Correggio, Van Dyck and Brueghel masterpieces. Of the three hundreds of the paintings hung at the Apsley House, only 83 remain.

The Duke of Wellington's house contained sculptures from Canova, an artist from the Venetian Republic City of Possagno who carved a statue for Napoleon at the French Emperor's request. An Italian neoclassical sculptor, Canova, was celebrated among the Venetian elite, with some of his work, including *Theseus and the*

Minotaur, showcased at the Victoria and Albert Museum. Canova had also carved statues of General George Washington and was highly praised by Catherine the Great, the Russian Enlightened despot, reflecting that these people, the great champions of the rational Enlightenment and revolution, all ran in the same circles.

Canova also completed a cenotaph, commemorating Clement XIII at St. Peter's Basilica. One cenotaph depicted Napoleon as Mars the Peacemaker. While Napoleon wanted to be displayed in his full French military regalia, Canova insisted that he be portrayed as "Mars," the father of Remus and Romulus – the mythical founder of Rome, in keeping with Rothschild plans to restore the Roman Empire with Rothschild heirs as hereditary dictators. Mars was also a pagan god who received sacrifices from Julian, an emperor who rejected Christianity. In the end, Napoleon was said to have felt betrayed, that he had been used as a mere puppet to serve secret agendas of which he was not fully aware.

Scattered throughout Wellington's townhouse were Venetian treasures, the Waterloo Shield, and a candelabra acquired from the Merchants of London. The architect was a Rothschild by the name of James Wyatt who presented him with a final bill for his work on the Apsley House in the amount of over £64,000, which the Duke of Wellington viewed as "an extortionate amount."

Wyatt had billed the Duke of Wellington three times more than the estimate, making "the sum so enormous that he did not know how to pay it." The celebrated military hero who led Britain to victory against Napoleon became Prime Minister in 1828, now indebted to the Rothschilds. They ensured that Wellington's home was decorated with the most glorious art work the world had to offer so that the Prime Minister would feel remain indebted to the dynasty and sufficiently malleable and agreeable to their self-serving demands. The Duke of Wellington was not so easily compromised.

In keeping with Venetian traditions, Wyatt had studied art and architecture in Venice with Antonio Visentini, who had measured the drawings for the dome of St. Peter's Basilica – and designed homes for the British Royal family. Wyatt also built Frogmore House near Windsor Castle, which was used by Queen

Victoria.

Listed among the Rothschilds' assets is Waddesdon Mansion, which showcases Leon Bakst's *Sleeping Beauty.* Commissioned by James de Rothschild, the painting was based upon an Italian fairy tale, *Sun, Moon, and Talia* written in 1634 by Giambattista Basile, a Venetian writer and courtier to Italian princes. In this tale, the King's daughter, Talia, was born with a divination that fated her to die from a splinter wound. Talia eventually fulfills the prophecy after attempting to help an old woman spin flax. In the process, a splinter is lodged under her fingernail, causing her to die instantly. A hunter then rapes her lifeless body.

Talia gives birth to twins while still unconscious but is awakened, briefly, when one of her sons suckles on her finger, pulling the splinter out. She calls the twins Sun and Moon, representing the dual nature of the occult, the yin and the yang. Upon awakening, the Queen becomes jealous of her and orders her to be thrown in a bonfire and sacrificed to Baal. The tale was immortalized in a Disney films and storybooks, and would mirror a Rothschild practice of drugging women and raping them to produce Rothschild heirs, as reported by Royal insiders.

Waddesdon Manor is graced with wall panels "taken from the homes of French aristocrats of the French revolutions." Its dining room contains mirrors and marble that "invoke the (Palace of Versailles)," the home of the French Monarchs executed during that Revolution. Four hundred piece of porcelain that serve 24 people can be found in the mansion as can treasures from King Louis XV; a carpet taken from the Palace of Versailles; and a desk made for Queen Marie Antoinette, who was beheaded by guillotine during the French Revolution. Rothschild's Waddesdon Manor at Buckinghamshire stands as a testament to Rothschild pillaging and social climbing into the aristocracy.

In 1817, Austria granted the dynasty its first coat of arms, elevating the Rothschilds to the status of "nobility," permitting them to use "von" in their name by the Order in Council of Francis I.

This honor was granted after Solomon Rothschild financed Kaiser Ferdinand's Nordham rail links, Austria's first steam railway, and other government projects.

The design for the Rothschild coat of arms is separated into four quadrants including: an eagle (representing Imperial and Royal Austrians); a leopard (representing English Royalty); a lion (representing their Hessian conquest); and a hand clutching five arrows (a symbol of the unity among the five brothers).

In 1818, the Rothschilds awarded themselves a British coat of arms. Four years later, the Rothschilds were granted the title of "Baron" through Austrian Imperial Decree. Ironically, their family motto was "*Concordia, Integritas, Industria*" (Harmony, Integrity, Diligence).

The Napoleonic Wars destroyed much of Europe, including the Holy Roman Empire. Salons, an Italian invention of the 16th century, popped up around Europe. Heralded as intellectual social get-togethers for the elite, salons promoted the principles of the rational Enlightenment, often drawing in well meaning people inspired by the lofty principles of fairness, equity, and representative governments.

As the Rothschilds sought to topple governments throughout Europe, over 50 countries succumbed to revolution in 1848, with tens of thousands of lives lost in the madness.

The following year, the East India Company established a gentleman's man (https://www.eastindiaclub.co.uk/) at 16 St James's Square in London, which was once occupied by Robert Villiers, 3rd Viscount Purbeck, the brother of King James' homosexual lover, John Villiers. According to the EIC's 1851 rule book, the club's members included "The East India Company's servants – Clerical, Civil, Military, Naval and Medical of all the Presidencies, including those retired (and) all commissioned officers of Her Majesty's Army and Navy who have served in India, members of the Bar and Legal Profession who may have been or are Company's Advocates and Solicitors."

The EIC has reciprocal clubs in the United Kingdom, Australasia, Africa, Europe, Asia, the Middle East, and America and the Caribbean, including, for example, the Cosmos Club in Washington, DC; the Standard Club in Chicago, Illinois; and the Minneapolis Club in Minneapolis, Minnesota, to name a few.

After the French Monarchy rejected the rational Enlightenment, Rothschild's rent-a-mob peasants spontaneously took to the streets to overthrow King Louis Philippe. Within three years, Napoleon Bonaparte's nephew arrived on the scene to suspend the elected assembly and establish the Second French Empire. Napoleon III became France's last monarch. After waging war against Prussia, Napoleon III was captured, dethroned, and exiled to England.

Napoleon then traveled to the United States to meet New York's literati, including a famous writer by the name of Washington Irving, who authored *Rip Van Winkle,* the story of a Dutch-American colonist who sleeps through the American Revolution only to awaken to find an entirely new world.

Irving, who had been commissioned to write books for the Astor family, despaired over the corruption he had witnessed during his literary junkets: "I am wearied and at times heartsick of the wretched politics of this country. The last ten or twelve years of my life has shown me so much of the dark side of human nature, that I begin to have painful doubts of my fellow man; and look back with regret to the confiding period of my literary career, when, poor as a rat, but rich in dreams, I beheld the world through the medium of my imagination and was apt to believe men as good as I wished them to be."

God's Intervention

As revolution burned through Europe, Christian Monarchs joined forces to douse the flames that were consuming the continent. Between 1814 and 1815, Austria, France, Russia, and England convened the Congress of Vienna to challenge populist demands for "representative government, freedom, and liberty." Most citizens were led to believe that Monarchies represented tyranny and reactionary policies and that Venetian-inspired reforms were opening the world up to a new era of freedom, progress, and human rights. The reality is that a moral people do not need external controls to do right or to live freely. Rather, those controls come from within. Only when chaos reins does tyranny need to be imposed from without to restore and maintain order.

As God was removed from the public square, society naturally degenerated, allowing corrupt elites to pander to human nature's worst instincts and encourage debauchery and rebellion and replace dedication to God, family, and country with the pursuit of wealth, power, and pleasure at the expense of all else.

The Christian Monarchs attempted to restore Christian virtue after Napoleon tried to eradicate it from the lands he conquered. In the wake of widespread rebellion and chaos that stood to destroy society at its foundation, Christian Monarchs imposed dictatorial controls and censorship, but this was not intended to muzzle free speech or oppress citizens, but to stifle the toxic propaganda and criminality the Venetians were spewing under the cloak of endless self-serving virtue signaling that was leading to murder, revolution and the destruction of society.

The Holy Alliance united Christian Monarchs to oppose the revolutions by neutralizing the Venetian influence in the United States and elsewhere. The Monarchs signed the Treaty of Verona in 1822 in response to the Monroe Doctrine. While historians portray the Monroe Doctrine as a noble effort to protect the United States and Latin America from foreign meddling, the reality is that this policy was inspired by Rothschild efforts to separate colonies in North and South America from their European empires so that the dynasty could install puppet governments, foment revolutions, plunder natural resources and wealth, and enslave and otherwise exploit people for their profit and pleasure.

With this agenda in mind, the Rothschilds directed their agents in the United States to respond to the Treaty of Verona "with the Vatican's interests at heart." The Treaty was portrayed as an attempt by the European Monarchs to enslave Americans and deprive them of their democratic rights and republican form of government so that a shadow elite could impose despotism upon the country. The reality was the opposite. By Rothschild's own admission, the Holy Alliance took aim at the "works of Satan."

Written by James Monroe, a Founding Father inspired by the rational Enlightenment, the Monroe Doctrine sought to curtail any foreign intervention in America's sphere of influence. To understand where Monroe was coming from, during the American Revolution, Monroe stormed the Palace of the Governor, where a representative to the British Monarchy resided. This was his "storming the Bastille" moment.

While Monroe made the rounds, promoting liberty, equality, and fraternity, he was a slave-owner who attacked British agents in the colonies who had attempted to free slaves and end the profitable East India Company's slave trade.

Alexander Hamilton recruited Monroe to join the Continental Army, and then Thomas Jefferson recruited him to fight in the American Revolution. All three were Rothschild agents. As a colonel, Monroe established a "messenger network," based upon the Venetian spy model, to coordinate the Continental Army with other state militias. After he studied law under Jefferson, he provided aid and comfort to French revolutionaries.

As Minister Plenipotentiary to France, Monroe lobbied to have British agitator Thomas Paine and the wife of Marquis de Lafayette, a French aristocrat who fought in the American Revolution, released from prison. If the American Revolution were about ending the British Monarch's meddling in colonial affairs and restoring power to the people, why were so many aristocrats supporting the effort that most colonialist did not even want to join? The fact is that the revolution was not about empowering the people, but about facilitating the private theft of American assets and resources while attempting to reorder society under Rothschild control.

After writing *The Declaration of the Rights of Man* with Jefferson's assistance, de Lafayette was captured by Austrian troops for subversive activities only to be released from prison at Napoleon's direction. Upon returning to the United States, Monroe entertained de Lafayette as a celebrity.

The Declaration of Rights of Man gave hint to Venetian subversion. For example, Article III states that "no individual may exercise any authority which does not proceed directly from the nation." This article reflects the rational Enlightened view that rights are not conferred by God, but the nation, which was controlled by powerful special interests. Article VI affirms that "the law is the expression of the general will" and that the law must be "the same for all, either that it protects or that it punishes," reflecting yet another hollow argument of the proponents of the rational Enlightenment who established a two-tired justice system in which those with political influence, wealth, and power could skirt the law while the less well off were often subjected to arbitrary judgments. Justice was never blind under their new republican governments.

The *Declaration* also affirms that "free communication of thoughts and opinions is one of the most precious rights of man." Yet the Venetian controllers have repeatedly used free speech to misinform, malign, mock, defame, intimidate and propagandize while stifling the free speech of others. Even though the *Declaration* affirms that property is an "inviolable and sacred right," the proponents of the rational Enlightenment have stripped away property through confiscatory taxation, outright theft, and now through the "Great Reset," a world in which people will somehow be happy by owning nothing. However, as the revolutionaries affirmed from the beginning, what is sacred and inviolable one day may not be the next.

As the Americans grew disenchanted with their new republic, Monroe enlisted de Lafayette to sell the Americans on the idea of a republic while the Rothschilds manufactured the Panic of 1819 to create a financial crisis that would collapse the economy and whip the people back into line. The panic led to excessive land speculation and unrestrained spending though central banks.

Ever wise to the wiles of foreign interests, President George Washington concluded that Monroe was not to be trusted. Not only did Monroe oppose the ratification of the U.S Constitution but he attempted to use a militia to secure victory for Jefferson in an election. Monroe led the charge to establish Virginia's first penitentiary to imprison dissenters. As Governor of Virginia, he dispatched the militia to put down a slave rebellion, hung rebellious slaves for treason, and then attempted to banish slaves on conspiracy and treason charges for resisting their enslavement and seeking freedom, reflecting the true values of the rational Enlightenment.

As President, Monroe was sympathetic to the revolutionary movements in Latin America that enabled the Rothschilds to separate colonies from the European Monarchs and install puppet governments in their place. The official policy of the United States was to support republican institutions and seek most favored nation status to develop economic and political institutions that were democratic in appearance while secretly serving a corrupt shadow elite. Monroe claimed his policy was meant to set an example for "liberty and humanity" for the rest of the world, which is laughable on its face. A Presbyterian minister by the name of Renwick Wilson once observed that Monroe "lived and died like a second rate Athenian philosopher."

The Monarchs of Europe understood the revolutionary threat and sought to neutralize it. The Treaty of Verona declared that "a system of representative government is ... incompatible with monarchical principles" and that liberalism was opposed to the "high divine right." Congress was appalled to discover that an Alliance was "using all their efforts to put an end to the system of representative government, in whatever country it may exist in Europe and to prevent its being introduced in those countries where it is not yet known." Congressmen concluded that the Treaty was evidence of a secret agenda by elites to impose tyranny over free Americans

As the Holy Alliance affirmed: "It cannot be doubted that the liberty of the press is the most powerful means used by the pretend supporters of the rights of nations to suppress it, not only in their own states but also the rest of Europe." Recall that Benjamin Franklin had traveled to England to enlist Thomas Paine, a foreigner, to write pamphlets to distribute to the colonists to manufacture grievances that would drive them into war against England. While essential to a well functioning democracy, the free press was transformed into a weapon against the people. If knowledge is power, the secret controllers jealously held real knowledge for themselves while doing their utmost to keep the public ignorant and misinformed.

During the Revolution, Adam Weishaupt promised that subversive forces "will infiltrate (the Vatican), and that once inside we will never come out. We will bore from within until nothing remains but an empty shell." One year after the Treaty of Verona was signed, the Vatican was bankrupt and indebted to the Rothschilds. Pope Gregory XVI then honored Calman Rothschild with a Papal decoration for loaning the Vatican £5 million.

By the mid-1900s, the United States would once again be at war – this time over slavery. After the North defeated the South, with the Rothschilds financing both sides, the Holy Alliance intervened to prevent the dynasty from dividing up the country among themselves. At the same time, debt generated through war led the country into being perpetually indebted to the Vatican, British Crown, and Rothschilds.

In the ensuing decades, America's middle class would be decimated and the media and politicians would serve private interests at the expense of the public good. What ever happened to the much ballyhooed representative government?

Under the Petticoat

The moral decay seeping into the British Empire was apparent for all to see. Commenting on the corrupting Venetian influence, John Ruskin observed in the *Stone of Venice* that "Venice stands, from first to last, like a masked statue; her coldness impenetrable, her exertion only aroused by the touch of a secret spring (of) commercial interest – the one motive of all her important political acts, or enduring national animosities. She could forgive insults to her honor, but never rivalship in her commerce. All Europe around her was wasted by the fire of its devotion. She first calculated the highest price she could exact from its piety for the armaments she furnished, and then, for the advancement of her own private interests, at once broke her faith."

Ruskin observed that Pope Clement V had excommunicated Venetians and compared them to Lucifer. "Venice, as she was once the most religious, was in her fall the most corrupt of European states," he wrote. From the "corrupted papacy arose two great adversaries," the Protestants in Germany and England, and the rationalists in France and Italy, with the former "requiring the purification of religion," and the later, seeking "its destruction."

Dedicating to upholding public virtue and retaining the divine rights, Queen Victoria was coronated in 1837. A savvy and principled lady, the Queen was privy of Rothschild's efforts to extinguish the "divine rite" to rule and eradicate the legitimate Royal bloodline forever. In the interests of preserving the Royal blood line, she spent a small fortune researching the sacred Royal lineage.

In an effort to preserve the bloodline, she secretly married Prince George of Cumberland as a teen and gave birth to Prince Marcos Manoel. His legitimacy was recorded in a letter to her cousin, King Ferdinand II of Portugal, who announced "assemble him claimant" which was monogram sealed. water marked, and written in Queen Victoria's own handwriting. It also contained the DNA of her thumb print and blood. Marcus Manoel received the letter on St. Patrick's Day just before he turned 16.

Later Queen Victoria married her Prince consort, Albert, bigamously but had no children with him. Instead, Royal insiders say, she was drugged and raped by Lionel Nathan Rothschild who sired Rothschild bastard heirs who were married off to European monarchies. The marriages were arranged by Victoria's son, Edward ("Bertie") VII, a Rothschild bloodline, who would succeed her as Monarch.

In 1871, one daughter, Victoria Princess Royal, married Frederick III, the son of Wilhelm I. Together Frederick and Princess

Victoria ruled Germany and "liberalized" Europe. During their reign, German Chancellor Otto von Bismarck presided over British-style ministers who answered to the Reichstag, which was packed with "liberal" ministers. Liberalism was one of key agencies through which the Rothschilds sought to erode established power held by Christian rulers and create new republican governments they controlled.

Frederick III and Princess Victoria devoted themselves to "emancipating" German Jews. Taking a page out of the Rothschild playbook, Victoria and Frederick described anyone who complained of crimes committed in the name of Judaism as "lunatics of the most dangerous sort (who) belong in an insane asylum."

Frederick and Victoria even attended synagogue service in Venice "to demonstrate as clearly as we can what our convictions are." Frederick offered protection to the "poor, ill treated Jews" of Europe while ignoring the Venetians' poor treatment of these same people within Venice.

During his brief 99-day reign, Frederick issued an edict to limit the powers of the Chancellor and Monarch through a Venetian-style constitution that was never enacted.

While her illegitimate Royal children were wrecking havoc throughout Europe, Queen Victoria partnered with Russian Tsar Alexander II, her godfather who baptized her "Alexandrina Victoria," to establish a "Third Rome" in Russia to support and defend Judeo-Christianity in Europe.

Among the proponents of the Third Rome doctrine was Russian novelist and philosopher Vladimir Soloviev, who was active in the Society for the Promotion of Culture Among the Jews of Russia. Fluent in Hebrew, Soloviev sought to build bridges between Jews and Christians, reflecting that the natural state of affairs between Jews and Christians in Europe was one of harmony and friendship. He was also a defender of Jewish civil rights, leading *The Jewish Encyclopedia* to praise him as "a friend of the Jews (who) is said to have prayed for the Jewish people." At the same time, he supported ecumenicism – that is, uniting Christians in spiritual union under the leadership of Jesus Christ.

Soloviev's criticisms were reserved for the occultists. In his apocalyptic *Tale of the Antichrist,* which was subtitled *A Fable of the Deceiver,* he warned of an evil force spreading through Europe which sought to conquer Christian Russia. The force was characterized as "Pan-Mongolism – the unification of all the races of Eastern Asia with the aim of conducting a decisive war against foreign intruders, that is, against Europeans." The Mongolians were the mercenaries of the Venetian armies who drew their power from their occult and through rituals that sought to cast "a new Mongolian yoke" over Europe.

In his description of the Antichrist, the warrior-king, Soloviev wrote: "Satan fills his son with his spirit; his soul is filled with a glacial abundance of enormous power, courage, and effortless skill. He composes a manifesto, *The Open Path to World Peace and Welfare,* an all-embracing program that unites all contradictions in itself--the highest degree of freedom of thought and a comprehension of every mystical system, unrestricted individualism and a glowing devotion to the general good. He establishes a European union of states, then a world monarchy, satisfies the needs of all the poor without perceptibly affecting the rich and founds an inter-confessional institute for free biblical research. He seeks to be elected by the general assembly of the churches as head of the Church (from now on ecumenically united), and receives the approval of the majority....The spokesmen of Christianity are persecuted and killed, but they rise again; the last Christians journey to the wilderness, the Jews raise a revolt, and the Christians join with them. They are slaughtered; but then Christ appears, robed in the imperial purple, his hands outspread with the marks of the nails upon them, to rule for a thousand years with those who are his own."

The Satanic deceiver, he said, promises freedom but delivers enslavement; preaches universal rights while imposing tyranny; stokes revolution and war before offering world government for peace; creates scarcity and offers poisoned abundance. The deceivers are radicals, reformers, and revolutionaries who promise enlightenment, peace, and prosperity only to deliver destruction, poverty, and eternal darkness.

The Antichrist is the ultimate deceiver who pretends to be what he is not. He offers a "manifesto" through which "powerful imperialist parties are formed which compel their governments to join the United States of Europe under the supreme authority of the Roman Emperor," Soloviev said. The dream of the Antichrist ruling over all humanity was nursed and shared by the Rothschilds.

By the 19th century, the English Rothschilds became part of the political establishment. In 1858, following a long campaign, Lionel de Rothschild became the first Jewish MP, representing the City of London, to take his seat without the obligation of swearing an oath as a Protestant. While he portrayed his success as a great victory over antisemitism, Jews were not barred from higher office; they simply needed to pledge an oath to a government which served a Christian Monarchy that was under assault from the Vatican and other forces. Jews had long enjoyed position to influence with Britain, some even obtaining prominent positions that eluded Christians.

Another Rothschild, the liberal imperialist Archibald Primrose, 5th Earl of Rosebery, became British Secretary of State for Foreign Affairs and later, Prime Minister. His wife was Hannah de Rothschild, the sole heiress to Mayer Amschel de Rothschild's fortune. The product of nepotism, Lord Rosebery was widely viewed as an unaccomplished failure. He wrote biographies of famous Rothschild bloodlines and agents, including Napoleon Bonaparte and Lord Randolph Churchill.

Lionel Rothschild's son, Alfred Charles Freiherr de Rothschild, who worked at the N.M Rothschild Bank in New Court of London, became the first Jewish director of the Bank of England. In this role, he represented the British Government at an International Monetary Conference in Brussels, the capital of what was to become the European Community (European Union) as the Rothschild dynasty pressed forward to recreate the Roman Empire with themselves as dictators. Alfred's management was reportedly so disastrous that the Bank refused to allow another Jew to preside over the Bank for 50 years, which is regrettable considering the many talented Jewish bankers who would have performed the job brilliantly. The Rothschilds had once again given Jews a bad name.

The Rothschilds entertained Queen Victoria at Waddesdon Mansion and 'loaned' Queen Victoria and her consort, Prince Albert, funds to purchase the lease at Balmoral Castle and its 10,000 acres. Lionel was succeeded by his son, Nathaniel, or Natty, who as head of the London House of Rothschild, became the richest man in the world. Queen Victoria named 'Natty' the first Jewish peer.

Queen Victoria was a savvy Monarch who attempted to preserve morality and retain the legitimate blood line and initiation rites for the "divine rite" to rule. At her funeral, Queen Victoria was described as the matriarch of the "Venetian Black Guelphs/Black Nobility," with the nobles now conceding they would have to go into business" with the commoners in order to survive. Despite the glorious titles the Rothschilds acquired for themselves, they were still commoners, pirates, thieves, and pretenders to the throne who held influence and power through "color of law."

Queen Victoria characterized her illegitimate heir, Edward VII, a Rothschild bastard, in personal letters as being "very weak and terribly frivolous." She also lamented, "Oh! What will become of the poor country when I die! I foresee, if (Bernie) succeeds, nothing but misery – for he never reflects or listens for a moment and he (would) … spend his life in one whirl of amusements as he does. It makes me very sad and angry."

As a Rothschild bloodline, little was required of Edward beyond service to the dynasty. The more morally comprised and intellectually weak he turned out to be, the easier he would be to control. The dynasty bankrolled his bad habits as long as he remained useful. His devotion to the dynasty was so unquestioning and perverse that he attempted to have his own half-brother, the legitimate heir to the British throne, assassinated. As a reward for his faithful service, the Rothschilds covered Edward's gambling debts, ensuring that he lived in the lap of luxury despite lacking any discernible means of income. They also paid for his mortgage and covered the costs for his Royal estates at Balmoral and

Sandringham, explaining, perhaps why the Queen of England today, despite being one of the richest women in the world, lives on rations and is forced to use energy-efficient light bulbs in her castles.

The exiled king, Manuel II, referred to as "The Patriot" and "The Unfortunate," ascended the throne after Edward arranged the assassination of his father, King Carlos I, and his eldest brother, Luis Filipe, the Prince Royal.

The Portuguese Monarchy ended with another Venetian-inspired coup in 1910. Afterward, Manuel was exiled to Hampton Court Palace in London. The wealthy Vanderbilt family modeled their mansion in Florham in Madison, New Jersey on the palace's baroque architecture. The palace was also used as a venue for Disney's *Cinderella* and such movies as HBO's ministry, *John Adams,* and *To Kill a King.*

As an illegitimate heir, Edward served a predatory dynasty over the interests of the British people, reflecting how negatively the usurpation impacted Britain and the world. For example, in 1890, Edward issued an ultimatum to Portugal which forced Portuguese military forces to retreat from areas claimed by Portugal, whose Royals were related to the legitimate British Royal family. The Rothschilds wanted those tracks of land, including Mozambique – and Angola where the Rothschilds planned to mine for diamonds. The ultimatum was one of the main causes of the revolution which ended the Monarchy in Portugal 20 years later.

The House of Rothschild lavished money upon compliant politicians, like Randolph Churchill, another Rothschild bloodline and father of Prime Minister Winston Churchill, who in his capacity as Secretary of State for India, annexed Burma as a New Year's present for Queen Victoria. The Rothschilds reaped the profits from Burma's ruby mines, not Queen Victoria or the British citizens.

As Edward VII prepared to assume the throne, the Rothschilds formed a secret society called the Round Table as they tightened their control over the British Empire and expanded the areas over which they wanted to rule. In order to retain their illegitimate position and keep their ill gotten gains, the Rothschilds surrounded themselves with a network of allies who would defend and advance Rothschild interests in exchange for a taste of the good life and the trappings of wealth and power. Typically the Rothschilds allowed their helpers to enjoy prestige and affluence as a reward for their service only to claw back those gains years later once the helper had outlived his usefulness. The legacy of such helpers would be determined by the value of their service, with those the Rothschilds wished to remember favorably receiving favorable press coverage while those who had fallen out of favor were maligned in the most despicable fashion.

A key player within Rothschild's secret society was Cecil Rhodes, a young man who became rich mining diamonds for Rothschild's De Beers company in Africa. De Beers was modeled after the East India Company. After becoming fabulously rich through his Rothschild associations, Rhodes sought to advance British imperialism through Rhodes Scholarships. Among the goals of the scholarship was to recover the United States as a colony for Great Britain, except this time, the country would be reduced to a bankrupt welfare state that provided a military for Rothschild wars, funding for Rothschild projects, and wage slaves to fund an empire.

Scholarships were given to promising American students so that they could study abroad for a year at the University of Oxford and become indoctrinated in Rothschild's world view. Once they returned to the United States, Rhodes Scholars would reach positions of great influence and wealth and take actions throughout their lives to advance the agenda. The wealth that Rhodes had accumulated working for Rothschild was used to benefit the dynasty exclusively, with Rothschild serving as executor of the wills and trustees of his estate.

Rothschild also used the secret societies to promote Zionism to acquire British Palestine so that the dynasty could claim Jerusalem and rule the world from Israel, a longstanding Venetian goal. Most of the Round Table members, who seemed oblivious to wider Rothschild agenda, proposed that Jews be given land in Africa that was not populated or developed so that they could build a country for Jews anew, without upsetting the Arabs or moving people off land that had been claimed by others. This land could be developed from scratch and be exclusively Jewish from the start.

In 1924, Baron Edmond de Rothschild established the Palestine Jewish Colonization Association, known as PICA. Originally a branch of the Jewish Colonization Association set up in 1891 to support Jewish settlers displaced from Russia, Baron Edmond de Rothschild donated land and considerable funds in 1899 to subsidize 19 of 23 settlements in Palestine for Jews fleeing antisemitism.

Through King Edward VII, the Rothschilds had the Monarch's support for the Balfour Declaration that promised Palestine to the Rothschilds. The Round Table then solicited a declaration written by Foreign Secretary Arthur Balfour, the Duke of Wellington's godson, for Lord Rothschild, affirming the British Government's support of a Jewish homeland in Palestine. At Rothschild's behest, Chaim Weizmann, a Russian chemist, was dispatched to lobby the British Government for the Balfour Declaration, though this was likely done for show since the dynasty had most, if not all, of the key decision makers in its pocket one way or the other.

Weizmann was a leading Zionist and Rothschild agent who presided over the Zionist Organization and attended the Second Zionist Congress in Basel. His family appeared to full of Rothschild agents. One sibling, Shmuel Weizmann, was a dedicated Communist. Another, Maria Weizmann, was arrested in connection with Stalin's "doctors' plot," which involved having revolutionaries assassinate Soviet leaders so that the assassinations could be blamed on Jews to inspire violent attacks against the Jewish people to increase public support for a Jewish state. Another sibling was sleeping with a Nazi diplomat while the Nazis were exterminating the Jews and enforcing Nuremberg laws.

After acquiring British citizenship with the help of Winston Churchill, Weizmann promptly renounced it to become President of Israel.

Rothschild's Round Table set the stage for the World Wars, which launched the new world order. As Gerry Docherty and Jim MacGregor wrote in *The Hidden History: The Secret Origins of the First World War*: "Far from sleep walking into a global strategy, the unsuspecting world was ambushed by a secret cabal of warmongers in London with the long-term aim of taking control of the entire world. These individuals, whom we call the secret elite, deliberately fomented the Boer War of 1899–1902 in order to grab the Transvaal's gold mines, and this became a template for their future actions. Their ambition overrode humanity, and the consequences of their actions have been minimized, ignored, or denied in official histories. The horror of the British concentration camps in South Africa, where 20,000 children died, is conveniently glossed over; the devastating loss of a generation in a World War. They had the power to control history, to turn history from enlightenment to deception. (They) dictated the writing and teachings of history, from the ivory towers of academia down to the smallest of schools. They carefully controlled the publication of official government papers, the selection of documents for inclusion in the official version of the history of the First World War, and refused access to any evidence that might betray their covert existence. Incriminating documents were burned, removed from official records, shredded, falsified or deliberately rewritten, so that what remained for genuine researchers and historians was carefully selected; soldiers have been glorified by the lie that they died for freedom and civilization. (This) cabal of international bankers, industrialists, and their political agents successfully used war to destroy the Boer Republics and then Germany, and were never called to account."

Towards the end of the 19th century, the Rothschilds remained obsessed with German power, which they feared would eclipse their own. Germany made incredible advances in science and technology, outpacing Britain in industrial output. While Germany was investing in research and development, the British were wasting their precious resources on endless Rothschild-inspired wars for empire that depleted the national reserves and overextended the empire. By some estimates, Britain waged over 100 wars during the reign of Queen Victoria, who was sympathetic towards the Germans, given the familial connections through the House of

Saxe-Coburg-Gotha.

Once her son, Edward, came of age, he engaged in a level of shuttle diplomacy worthy of Henry Kissinger or Hillary Clinton. As Rothschild agent, he traveled from country to country to secure foreign support for Rothshchild plans, starting with the destruction of Germany. Edward's wife, Princess Alexandra of Denmark, enjoyed a close relationship with the Tsarina of Russia who had married Tsar Nicholas II. The Russians had fallen into debt to Rothschild after borrowing 400 million francs to construct the Trans-Siberian Railways so Russia could transport armies by rail and expand trade between Moscow and the Far East. As a gesture of gratitude for the loan, the Tsar awarded Alphonse de Rothschild the Grand Cross. The Rothschilds reciprocated in kind by financing a revolution to topple the Tsar.

Through Edward's mediation, the Rothschilds extracted a commitment from Russia to wage war against Germany over promises that it would be granted control of Constantinople and the Black Sea Straits. This concession was appealing to supporters of the Third Rome who sought to recover the Christian city of Constantinople for the Christian people. Constantinople also provided a warm-water port and an unrestricted naval outlet to the Mediterranean.

As could have been anticipated, Rothschild reneged on his promises to Russia. The Anglo-Russian Convention signed on August 31, 1907 focused on Persia, Afghanistan and Tibet, without even mentioning Constantinople. By 1914, over 80 per cent of Russian debt was owed to French banks which demanded that Russia increase its military and modernize its rail system to attack Germany. The Rothschilds dominated French banking and worked with the House of Rothschild in London and Paris to secure loans for Russia.

Once the Round Table was up and running, London had reinforced its position as the world's greatest financial center and lender of choice for governments and companies. Politicians were bought off, bankers and corporate executives were enriched, and the world's wealth and power were increasingly consolidated within the hands of a few, including American industrialists and bankers, like the Rockefellers, Fords, Carnegies, Morgans, DuPonts, among others who served as fronts and agents for the Rothschild agenda.

In 1903, Sir Edward Grey, a British foreign secretary, launched an expedition to Tibet to establish diplomatic relations and resolve a border dispute. Led by Francis Younghusband, a military mission was dispatched to Tibet to establish an Anglo-Tibetan Convention as the shadow elite planned to unleash a brutal attack on the European continent steeped in the occult practices that would cost tens of millions of people their lives and devastate Europe. With God removed from society, there was no amount of evil that was off limits as the Rothschild advanced toward their goals of restoring the Roman Empire, reestablishing ancient Venetian trade routes, and elevating Communist China to leader of a new world order of tyranny.

IV.
Blasphemous Butchery

At the start of World War I, Europe was ruled by Rothschild bloodlines and agents. The dynasty was thus able to influence countries as if they were mere pawns on a chessboard. The last Romanov Tsar, Nicholas II of Russia, was the cousin of German Kaiser Wilhelm II, who was Queen Victoria's grandson. Both Wilhelm and Nicholas were third cousins who shared a common ancestor in Frederick William III of Prussia, the great-great-great grandson of Paul I of Russia, the son of Catherine the Great, an Enlightened despot. With the Rothschilds now in control of the British Monarchy, the dynasty sought to purge the last vestiges of legitimate Royal bloodlines.

After Russian Tsar Catherine the Great assassinated her husband, her son, Paul I, became the legitimate heir to the Romanov dynasty, but in true Enlightened despotic fashion, Catherine pushed her son aside to rule in his place. Paul was only able to claim the throne after her death. During his brief reign, Paul audited the Monarch's books and discovered that money was being stolen from the treasury. This led him to ask some uncomfortable questions. He also sought to grant rights to peasants instead of virtue signaling as his mother had done. The hidden hand wasn't about to tolerate a legitimate ruler, much less one who challenged its criminal behavior, and so he was assassinated in 1801 at St. Michael's Castle. Among the assassins was General Levin August von Bennigsen, a Hanoverian in the Russian service who worked closely with Catherine's advisors. The other assassin was General Vladimir Mikhailovich Yashvil of Georgia.

During the American Civil War, Russia intervened to prevent the Rothschilds from dividing up Judeo-Christian America. Presiding over Russia at the time was Tsar Alexander III who followed President Abraham Lincoln's decision to free the slaves by freeing Russian serfs, stating that he wanted no part in the enslavement of mankind. Alexander the Liberator, as he was known, also reorganized the judicial system, abolished corporal punishment, promoted local self government, imposed universal military service, ended privileges for the nobility, and promoted universal education. Afraid that Alaska would fall into the hands of the Rothschilds, Alexander sold the territory to the United States. The hidden hand rewarded Alexander III and Lincoln for their service to humanity by assassinating them both.

The brother of Russian Communist Party founder Vladimir Lenin, Alexander Ulyanov, worked with Narodnaya Volya, a terrorist group that organized the assassination of Tsar Alexander II and attempted to kill the Tsar's son and successor, Alexander III. After he was arrested, Ulyanov admitted his complicity while parroting rational Enlightenment talking points: "Terror is our answer to the violence of the state," he said. "It is the only way to force a despotic regime to grant political freedom to the people." While Alexander III was liberating the people, Rothschild was enslaving them. Ulyanov was executed by hanging. In true gangster style, Lenin promised to avenge his death.

After fleeing to the Gatchina Palace for safety reasons, Alexander III said: "To think that after having faced the guns of the Turks, I must retreat now before these skunks."

Alexander III murdered his other brother, Grand Duke Nicholas II so that he could claim the Russian throne for himself. After Alexander III died in 1894, his heir, the naive and gentle Nicholas III, became the last Romanov Tsar.

By this point, the Rothschilds and fellow international financiers had their hands in Russia's pockets. In addition to financing the Trans-Siberian railroad and other infrastructure projects, the dynasty loaned the Russian government money to develop oil fields around Baku. As the Russian empire expanded through rational Enlightened conquest, the country was drained of its resources.

Through loans and insurance schemes, the Rothschilds established intelligence networks throughout the countries in which they conducted business. The Paris Rothschilds raised money through bonds to develop Russia's railways and industry. Next to fall was Russia.

In 1903, aspiring revolutionary Vladimir Lenin organized the Russian Social Democratic Party, which convened in London where he was groomed for the historic role he would play on the world stage. Once he was sufficiently trained, the hidden hand helped Lenin form a Red Army to unleash a campaign of Red Terror against the Russians on behalf of the "proletarians" (workers), who were encouraged to rise up against the bourgeoisie to seize control of industry in typical Venetian slash, loot, and burn fashion, or what amounted to a replay of the French Revolution and the Revolutions of 1848.

The Red Army specifically targeted the White Army, which was comprised of Christian aristocrats, supporters of the Romanov dynasty, business people, intellectuals, and the deeply religious. In 1905, political uprisings, labor strikes, and terrorist attacks were fomented against the government of Russia, with financing provided by the Rothschilds and Jacob Schiff, a banker who had been linked with the Rothschilds since the 1800s.

The Schiff and Rothschild families had actually lived within the same building in the Jewish ghetto in Frankfurt am Main. Schiff would later establish Kuhn, Loeb & Co. Bank, an extension of the Rothschild banking empire. He also hired the infamous banker Paul Warburg.

In 1905, the Reds murdered the Grand Duke Sergie Alexandrovich, Tsar Nicholas III's uncle. The Grand Duke's wife, Duchess Elizabeth exited public life to establish a convent to help the poor. In 1918, the revolutionaries murdered the Duchess and her maid too. Within a span of four years, from 1905 to 1909, the Reds had killed thousands of people.

Tsar Nicholas II hoped to appease the revolutionaries by making concessions, perhaps not realizing that his enemies wanted nothing short of the complete overthrow the Russian Monarchy and the extermination of its Royal families. Every last drop of legitimate Royal blood needed to be spilled to satiate Rothschild power lust. In a misguided effort to appease the radicals, the Tsar signed the *October Manifesto* to establish a Venetian-style government, including an elected legislature (Duma) and new constitution so the Rothschilds could install their own puppet representatives.

The Tsar then purged Lenin and Trotsky, who fled to Switzerland and New York. Like a cockroach infestation, there was no getting rid of them. When the radicals returned, they were well funded, thanks to financial resources provided to them by international bankers and Wall Street. Lenin founded *Iskra* (the *Spark*), a publication that sought to ignite *The Blaze* – that is, Marxist revolution throughout the world.

In 1909, Lenin published his own Manifesto, *What is to be Done*, arguing that revolution should be undertaken by community organizers (trained revolutionaries) rather than workers. However, if the grievances over which he protested had merit, disgruntled peasants and proletarians would have joined his cause. Since these revolutions were principally concerned with amassing money and power for the unprincipled criminals waging them, the revolutionaries were forced to recruit from their own ranks. "Socialist consciousness cannot exist among the workers," Lenin complained. "This can be introduced only from without."

Lenin reached out to Alexander Israel Helphand, a Russian-German Marxist who grew up in Odessa, a city that Catherine the Great had founded by decree as an important trading port and naval base. Helphand helped Lenin return to Russia in a "sealed train" to launch the Revolution in 1917.

As leader of the Bolsheviks, Lenin led the proletarian struggle against Tsarist Russia, replete with political assassinations, pogroms, peasant rebellions, and bloody massacres.

Tsar Nicholas II had the misfortune of marrying the German-born Empress, Alexandra from Hesse. While Nicholas was away putting down rebellions within Russia, his German-born wife, Alexandra, was inviting the enemy into their ranks - a radical peasant from Siberia by the name of Gregory Rasputin who was allowed to weigh in on policy and make recommendations that weakened the Monarchy. Alexandra was Queen Victoria's granddaughter, another product of the secret Rothschild breeding program.

The Tsar presided over the Trans-Siberian Committee to establish a Rothschild-financed railroad, perhaps not realizing that the dynasty was plotting his assassination.

Meanwhile, Joseph Stalin, a Rothschild bloodline trained at London's Tavistock Institute, was being groomed to lead revolution and continue Catherine's modernization efforts. Stalin joined Lenin's efforts by fomenting rebellions and strikes.

Nicholas II responded to Stalin's rebellions by directing troops to kill hundreds of protesters who had congregated at the Winter Palace. Stalin then claimed to be the victim, complaining that "the government has trampled on and mocked our human dignity."

A Rothschild plant, Stalin wanted nothing short of overthrowing the Tsar and establishing a Soviet dictatorship. Revolution was therefore inevitable. "It is just as inevitable as the sunrise," he said. "Russia is a loaded gun at full cock, liable to go off at the slightest concussion. Yes, comrades, the time is not far off when the revolution will hoist sail and drive the vile throne of the despicable Tsar off the face of the earth."

To this end, Stalin formed secret Bolshevik Battle Squads who raided and burned government` arsenals, attacked police, extorted money, robbed banks, and executed suspected traitors to the movement. He also founded and edited the communist newspaper called *Pravda* (or *Truth*), arguing that the newspaper would be key to "consolidating the underground hearts of the power." Newspapers, Lenin said, "should be not only be a collective agitator but a collective organizer."

In 1917, Lenin overthrew the Russian Monarchy and led the Bolshevik coup, sparking a civil war that resulted in the deaths of millions of people. "We must put an end once and for all to the papist-Quaker babble about the sanctity of human life," fumed Red Army founder Leon Trotsky.

Once the dust had settled, Democratic Socialist Alexander Kerensky, a Russian lawyer and revolutionary who played a key role in the Russian Revolution, joined a newly formed Russian Provisional Government, first as Minister of Justice and then as

Minister of War and then as second Minister Chairman. Kerensky was a leader of a moderate socialist faction of the Socialist Revolutionary Party and Vice Chairman of the Petrograd Soviet. His government was overthrown by the Lenin-led Bolsheviks, who were thought to have gone underground.

The Romanov family gathered in Alexander Palace where they expected to be escorted to their private railway station and taken to safety. The train bore the flag and insignia of the Red Cross. Once the family boarded the train, they were taken to a cellar where Tsar Nicholas III, Alexandra, and their four daughters and one son were placed under house arrests, lined up against a wall, and brutally shot. Nicholas II had hoped to be exiled to Great Britain while Kerensky was in power, but his first cousin, King George V, the illegitimate son of Tsar Alexander, refused to intervene to rescue him over concerns that offering him refuge would spark revolution in Britain.

The bloodlines whose blood had been tainted by Rothschild inbreeding seemed, at times, oblivious to the fact that the Rothschilds, who were advising them, were behind the unrest and chaos they were experiencing within their own countries. Information was shared on a need-to-know basis. Keeping Monarchs in the dark prevented them from acting in their own interests and intervening to help their relatives from being massacred. Since many were illegitimate, their positions were tenuous at best, reducing many to mere puppets on the world stage. Perhaps if enough people had been aware of the machinations and were willing to speak about them, the Rothschilds would have met the same fate they meted out to their enemies and the world would have been spared much suffering.

Once the beautiful Romanov family was executed, their art collections were "rescued" by Bolsheviks bankrolled by wealthy industrialists. Peter the Great had established the Diamond Fund to sustain the Romanov dynasty for generations. Based upon the terms of the trust, the treasures were not to be sold or given away. In fact, every generation of Romanovs was expected to add to the fund. Before their execution, the Romanov dynasty was among the wealthiest families in the world. By today's standards, the Romanovs were worth $280 billion. The Diamond Fund included a collection of crowns, orbs, diadems, tiaras, necklaces, bracelets and other adornments. The Bolsheviks seized the treasure and sold it to raise money for the revolution.

Many Romanov treasures were sold and auctioned off at Christie's and Sotherby's and inventoried for sale by the Soviets. Among those who purchased Romanov treasures was Armand Hammer, an American business owner who presided over Occidental Petroleum. Hammer was renowned for his art collection, business interests around the world, and citizen diplomacy that helped him cultivate a wide network of friends and associates. Hammer's family, who immigrated from Odessa, was the inspiration behind the "arm and hammer" symbol that represents the Socialist Labor Party (SLP) of America in which his father played a leading role. After the Russian Revolution, the SLP established the Communist Party of the United States.

Hammer made the precious Romanov jewels and art available for purchase in his department stores in New York City, providing a valuable source of income for the Soviet government. Lenin sold Romanov treasures to purchase tractors, locomotives, and plow shares. He even brokered a deal with the British government that allowed him to buy advanced airplane engines from the Rolls Royce company, which provided him a 15 percent discount on his vehicles.

Another avid collector of stolen Romanov art was Marjorie Merriweather Post, the heiress of the Post Cereal fortune who married American diplomat Joseph E Davis, the U.S. Ambassador to the USSR. Malcolm Forbes, the entrepreneur who founded *Forbes* magazine, proved to be a keen Romanov art collector as did U.S. Secretary of Treasury Andrew Mellon. While publicly supporting trade sanctions and embargoes between the United States and the Soviet Union, Mellon purchased 25 Romanov masterpieces from the Soviets in a private sale. *The Atlantic Constitution* reported that a delegation of American businessmen and wealthy collectors made a special trip to Russia to purchase the art and jewelry of the fallen Romanov family.

One can only wonder if these elites who lined their homes with Romanov treasures even paused for a moment to consider the screams of terror of the Romanovs before the Russian Royal family met its brutal death before a firing squad. As would later become clear, corporate America was heavily invested in Nazi Germany, the Soviet Union, and Communist China where profits were pursued with no consideration given to principle, values, or the human cost of doing business.

The Soviet Union rose from the ashes of Revolution. Once the USSR was established, Lenin nationalized industry and commandeered surplus food and grain for use by the Red Army, resulting in widespread famine. Communist policies predictably failed to help the plight of the poor – a fact that is not surprisingly considering that the poor were only a means to an end. In response to rising public resistance, Lenin launched the New Economic Policy as a limited free market system based upon capitalist ideas but which was subject to state control. To consolidate power, he banned all parties and factions except for the Communist Party. All political opposition and dissenting speech were outlawed, eerily reminiscent of the efforts by Big Tech companies to deplatform all voices critical of the globalist agenda, with Communist China dictating the acceptability of content.

The Rothschilds launched World War I to bring America into the war to weaken Germany, with Lenin affirming that "the European and World War has the clearly defined character of a bourgeoisie, imperialist, and dynastic war – a struggle for markets and for freedom to loot foreign countries, a striving to suppress the revolutionary movement of the proletariat and democracy in the individual countries, a desire to deceive, disunite, and slaughter the proletarians of all countries by setting the wage slaves of one nation against those of another so as to benefit the bourgeoisie – these are the only real content and significance of war."

In 1918, the Communist International (Comintern) was launched to fight "by all available means, including armed force, for the overthrow of the international bourgeoisie and for the creation of an international Soviet republic," or world government, a longstanding goal of the rational Enlightenment and the Rothschilds. After its ignominious launch, Comintern opened offices throughout the world in countries where the Rothschilds had already established a presence, including, for example, France, Italy, China, Germany, Spain, Belgium, and the United States. All took orders from a central authority – the Soviet Union, which was bankrolled by Wall Street, with the Rockefeller dynasty in the United States setting the stage to establish its headquarters in the Kremlin while the Rothschilds planned for their own in Israel. As Secretary of State, Henry Kissinger would later try to pit the Soviet Union and Communist China against each other as a divide-and-conquer strategy to destroy them both for imperial conquest.

In 1918, Lenin signed the Treaty of Brest-Litovsk with Imperial Germany, which ended Russia's participation in World War I. In the process, he surrendered much of the country's land and Russian population to Germany, which was presided over by Kaiser Wilhelm II, a Rothschild bloodline who would transform Germany into an even greater menace.

By this point, it was futile for Lenin to fight on as the Tsar's generals refused to support the Bolsheviks, resulting in mutinies and desertions within the ranks. Lenin's poorly trained Bolsheviks were undisciplined and lackluster. A Venetian-style snitch/spy network known as the Cheka then emerged to arrest, torture, and exterminate suspected traitors in a brutal Bolshevik purge. Those who betrayed Russia were among the first to go, with the Bolsheviks concluding that if one's loyalties could so easily be compromised, their support for the Bolsheviks would be tenuous at best.

After Lenin died in 1924, his successor, Joseph Stalin, consolidated control over the Communist Party and then imposed dictatorship, with the country undergoing rapid industrialization and forced collectivization. At the same time, the population was weakened through manufactured famines and food shortages. The nation's resources were commandeered to support Rothschild's war machine and increase the size of the territory the dynasty controlled, regardless of the human cost. Executions without trial were commonplace as were mass shootings and the burning of villages.

A Rothschild bloodline, Stalin was born in Georgia, a key trading hub and military garrison in the Russian Empire along the Silk Road that oversaw the movement of commerce and armed forces. The territory was hotly contested by major powers and had fallen under the control of the Persians and the Ottoman Turks, at various points in history.

Stalin was educated at the Tbilisi Spiritual Seminary, a spiritual training institution that operated between 1817 and 1919 in the Georgian "Exarchate," a governorship with military authority within the old Byzantine Empire. The exarch is the deputy of the patriarch who presides over the ministers. Tbilisi was of great strategic importance to the Byzantine and Venetian Empires since it was situated in the Caucasus between Europe and Asia, with Parthia, Sassanid Persia, Muslim Arabs, the Byzantine Empire, and Seljuk Turks all battling for control of this area.

The Seljuks were Turkic nomads who served in Khazar armies – armies so brutal, psychopathic, and utterly devoid of any moral scruples or humanity that the regional powers demanded that they convert to an Abrahamic religion or face extermination.

The Khazars chose Judaism, even though they never converted; the Seljuks eventually settled in Persia and converted to Sunni Islam.

Treasure the mercenaries acquired through conquest was horded in Tbilsi, which was sacked by Byzantine Khazar armies and later by Arabs, and then by the Khazars again, and then by Seljuk Turks.

These were the mercenary armies of the Venetian merchants whose corruption and psychopathy eventually felled the Venetian and Byzantine Empires while making their merchants exceedingly wealthy. The Mongols who served in these mercenary armies and were trading partners with the Venetian merchants invaded and conquered Tbilsi in the 13th century. Even though Tbilsi became semi-independent, the Mongolian influence shaped its government and culture. After the Mongolians left Georgia, Tbilisi became the capital of Georgia which then suffered an outbreak of the plague in what appears to be yet another instance of Venetian chemical warfare designed to exterminate the population so that its merchants could expand their living space and eliminate their rivals.

In 1801, the Russian Empire annexed the Georgian kingdom, with the Rothschilds and affiliated bankers helpfully offering to raise money to construct roads and railroads to connect Tbilisi with other key cities in the Russian Empire, such as Batumi and Poti, to provide a rail corridor linking Azerbaijan to Turkey via Georgia, thereby re-establishing and fortifying old Venetian trade routes. The English writer Rudyard Kipling observed at the time that Britain was dedicated to a "Great Game" against the old Ottoman and Russian Empires that involved plunging these areas into bloodbaths and war so that it could construct the Eurasian land-bridge-railroad and industrial development corridor lines, linking Beijing and the Far East to Europe and the Middle East, with the Rothschilds controlling Communist China and Great Britain.

Somehow despite studying at a "religious seminary," Stalin graduated as an atheist. As a young man, he read the complete works of William Shakespeare, reflecting the English influence upon his education. As a teenager, Stalin received financial support to complete his education by way of scholarship only to be expelled after missing his final exams. Stalin's failure to obtain a diploma would not impede his career plans.

After leaving school, Stalin found gainful employment at a Rothschild-owned oil refinery storehouse in Batumi. There he organized protests for the proletarians with the support of management. While studying Marxist theory in Georgia, he edited an underground Marxist newspaper called *Proletarian Struggle*. At the same time, he established a secret printing house with a hammer and sickle painted in a red circle on the front door and published leaflets, manifestos, and other publications that supported the Georgian Communist Party.

Writing under the name of Iosif Jugashvili, Stalin printed propaganda that called for the overthrow of Tsar Nicholas II before organizing strikes and revolution against the Romanov family who were eventually removed from power and executed by Rothschild-backed revolutionary forces. As the great Russian novelist Aleksandr Solzhenitsyn observed, the Russian Revolution waged on behalf of the proletarians was not even organically Russian, but imported from without by hostile forces. "You must understand," he said, "the leading Bolsheviks who took over Russia were not Russians. They hated Russians. They hated Christians. Driven by ethnic hatred, they tortured and slaughtered millions of Russians without a shred of human remorse. It cannot be overstated, Bolshevism committed the greatest human slaughter of all time. The fact that most of the world is ignorant and uncaring about this enormous crime is proof that the global media is in the hands of the perpetrators."

During his purges, Stalin targeted Christian intellectuals, forced church closures, and ordered the arrest of anyone found to have been practicing religion. Offenders were sent to the Gulag and executed; churches, mosques, and temples were destroyed while tens of thousands of monks, nuns, priests were martyred. At the same time, he attempted to categorize Soviet Jews under his nationality policy and create an alternate land for Israel with the help of Zomzet and OZET. Stalin proposed having the Jewish autonomous Olbast in the Russian Far East become the Soviet Zion, in the process destroying Jewish identity. Yiddish was to replace Hebrew as a Jewish language, and proletarian socialist literature and arts were to replace Judaism in Jewish culture.

He also colluded with Nazi Foreign Minister Joachim von Ribbentrop to banish Jewish intellectuals. He ordered his own Foreign Minister to "purge the ministry of Jews" before signing a non-aggression pact with Hitler, a fellow Rothschild bloodline. Many ethnic and religious Jews were purged under Stalin's regime and deported to Oblast and other parts of Siberia while those aligned with the shadow mercenary forces flourished and were promoted. Stalin, like other followers of the rational Enlightenment, condemned Christians as idolaters. He then erected statues of himself and promoted his own likeness as a kindly, but powerful, avuncular figure in propaganda literature so that others would worship him.

Stalin waged the Great Purge between 1936–1937. This time, over half a million Soviet citizens were executed as punishment for the crime of treason and terrorism against the Soviet regime. He also purged former opponents and Bolsheviks once they had outlived their usefulness, including members of the Soviet Communist Party. He directed peasants and workers to steal land and factories on behalf of the Communist Party. He then proceeded to oppress and exterminate them.

Stalin also supported Zionism on grounds that establishing a socialist country in the Middle East would weaken British influence there, clearing the way for Rothschild-affiliated companies to drill for oil and establish a base of power. Once these oil companies had been established, Secretary of State Henry Kissinger, an Anglo-Zionist agent, embarked on diplomatic missions throughout the globe with a view to ending U.S. energy independence and forging new energy markets in the Middle East upon which the United States would be dependent for oil, thereby allowing the country to be drawn into profitable wars for the Rothschilds. At the same time, the gold the Rothschilds had stolen from the United States and elsewhere could be sold to Middle Eastern countries while the dynasty controlled the price of gold through its gold exchanges in London, ensuring that the price was raised when oil-producing countries wanted to invest in gold and then lowered when they needed to sell it to raise capital. In the process, Kissinger established linkages and interdependencies among nations that made it difficult for countries to act within their own interests while the Rothschilds pulled the strings from the shadows as marionettes.

. Reminiscent of FEMA camps and the concentration camps built by Nazis, four large camps were built in southern and western Siberia for Jews. The deportations failed to take place as Stalin had died before the plan could be executed. The Deportation Commission had not yet compiled a complete list of all the Jews in the Russian territories. All "pure blood" Jews were slated to be deported first, followed by the "half-breeds," coinciding with the rise of Zionism in which Venetian mercenary forces were attempting to claim the Jewish identity for themselves so that they could rule the world from Jerusalem.

Historians have recorded that "at the time of Stalin's death, no Jew in Russia could feel safe." Stalin was even quoted as saying, "The good workers at the factory should be given clubs so they can beat the hell out of those Jews."

Between 1937 to 1938, Stalin purged 1.2 million people and ordered the execution of 40,000 more, stating "Who's going to remember all this riffraff in ten or 20 years time? No one!" – this coming from the mouth of a Rothschild bastard whose dynasty was founded in a Frankfurt ghetto and were themselves considered "riffraff" before they embarked on campaign to strip the world of its assets and put all of humanity under their thumb.

Among Stalin's cruelest schemes was his promotion of Holomodor in which he created the conditions for famine in the Ukraine to weaken the resolve of Ukrainian separatists. Millions died in of starvation. Stalin then seized private farms, reminiscent of efforts in the United States by Big Business (controlled by the Rothschilds) to move small farm owners off their land to make way for monopolies and the production of GMO foods, with leading global technocrat, Bill Gates, who has spoken of depopulating the world by 90 percent, buying up farm land. In desperation, starving Ukrainians succumbed to cannibalism after Stalin's military confiscated whatever food or livestock they had left.

The Blaze

The First World War (1914-18) was sparked after Archduke Franz Ferdinand of Austria, the heir to the Austria-Hungary Empire; and his wife, Duchess Sophie, were assassinated in Sarajevo, marking another assassination of Christian royalty. Notably, Archduke Ferdinand's older brother had joined the League of Three Emperors, who had formed a mutual defense pact against the Red menace.

Through this alliance, the Emperors promised to resolve differences through diplomacy rather than war, check British and French abuses of power, and squash radical plots to overthrow their governments. In other words, they had formed a power block to frustrate Rothschild plans.

During the First World War, Germany, Austria-Hungary, Bulgaria and the Ottoman Empire (the Central Powers) were pitted against Great Britain, France, Russia, Italy, Romania, Japan and the United States (the Allied Powers), with the Rothschilds controlling and financing both sides as part of a divide-and-conquer strategy. Once in place, the alliances set off a chain reaction that led to war.

Germany had never planned to fight, but suddenly Russian and French troops were amassing at its borders, forcing Germany to respond as London propagandists portrayed Germany as an aggressive, militaristic menace that needed to be subdued. By the end of the First World War, the German aristocracy would be eviscerated.

At the same time, war proved to be very profitable for many corporations, particularly multinationals, which became enriched through industry, military, and infrastructure projects for the European countries. The shadow elite destroyed these countries and then rebuilt them again, amassing a fortune through government contracts. By the end of the Second World War, over 16 million people had lost their lives and fortunes while the Rothschilds lived on to grow richer and ever more powerful.

With the Monroe Doctrine affirming American neutrality, Americans refused to be drawn into the dynastic wars raging on the European continent. Since the British needed to bring the United States into the War in order to crush Germany, a convincing argument needed to be crafted. To generate public support for war, the British media portrayed Germany as an existential threat to world peace.

Britain then coordinated the sinking of the Lusitania, a luxury passenger ship traveling from New York to Liverpool, England with hundreds of American passengers on board. As the ship approached the Irish coastline, the captain was directed to reduce speed, and then the military escort was withdrawn. Unbeknownst to the passengers, the ship was loaded with 600 tons of explosives, six million rounds of ammunition, and 1,200 cases of shrapnel. Aware that the city of London was attempting to use the sinking of the Lusitania as a pretext to bring the United States into war against Germany, the German Embassy attempted to warn the passengers by placing ads in American newspapers, but the newspapers refused to publish them.

Prime Minister Winston Churchill was fully aware of the situation and allowed a German torpedo to hit the munitions, causing an explosion to sink the ship in less than 20 minutes. Roughly 1,200 of the 2,000 passengers aboard the Lusitania perished. The Rothschild-controlled press then portrayed the attack as a German act of war against the United States, providing President Wilson the pretext he needed to join the Allies in 1914.

The Rothschilds were launching a multi-pronged attack against Germany from within and through external assaults by way of war. In 1915, Rosa Luxemburg and Karl Liebknecht founded the "Spartacus League" which became the Communist Party of Germany in recognition of Adam Weishaupt, who identified himself as "Spartacus." The Spartacists attempted to stage a coup in Berlin.

Leading Germany into World War I was Kaiser Wilhelm II, King Edward VII's nephew. As Queen Victoria's eldest grandson and a product of the secret Rothschild breeding program, Wilhelm was a frequent visitor to Osborne House on the Isle of Wight. There he visited the Royal British Navy headquarters at Portsmouth where he became interested in British warships and was promoted to British Admiral in 1889.

After receiving his British training, Wilhelm returned to Germany to upgrade the Navy so that it would overwhelm its British counterpart and be portrayed as a threat to British dominance. As Emperor, he pursued liberal reforms consistent with the Venetian rational Enlightenment. He also dismissed German Chancellor Otto von Bismarck so that he could pursue aggressive foreign policy through Weltpoltik. With deft diplomacy and military might, Wilhelm sought to secure Germany's "place in the sun." Instead of serving and defending the German people, Wilhelm aspired to be a dictator in the tradition of Napoleon. "The Reich has one ruler, and I am here," he said.

Throughout World War I, the Allies attempted to crush the Ottoman Empire so that they could wrestle Palestine from the Turks and claim it for the Rothschilds. Since 1882, the Zionists had planned to claim the Holy Land. In 1890, the Jewish Colonization Association was established to provide support for Jews fleeing Russian pogroms. In 1896, Theodor Herzl was inspired to write *The Jewish Case* after meeting the Rothschilds. That year, the Rothschilds targeted the Austrian-Hungarian empire for dissolution, with Herzl, an Austrian-Hungarian Jew, arguing at Basel that Palestine should be separated from the Ottomans. At first, the Zionists offered financial incentives in the form of reducing Turkey's foreign debt to Palestine if they would surrender the territory. The Turks refused this offer in 1901. The Rothschilds responded by subsidizing Jewish settlements. Two decades later, the dynasty founded the Palestine Jewish Colonization Association.

By the end of the First World War, the Ottoman and Austria-Hungarian Empires had fallen while Germany was identified as the source of all the trouble. In 1919, the Germans were forced to sign the Treaty of Versailles at the Paris Peace Conference, which was convened "to end all wars." Fearing the same fate at Tsar Nicholas, Kaiser Wilhem fled to Holland while denouncing the liberalism which had destroyed Germany.

Through peace negotiations, Germany was laden with heavy, punitive reparations, and hyperinflation. It was also denied entry into the League of Nations, a nascent world government established by the Rothschilds to keep the peace after the dynasty had fomented war.

Following the Armistice of 1918, the Rhineland was occupied by American, Belgian, British and French forces, with Germany forced to surrender the territory, thereby protecting Rothschild-affiliated multinationals, like I.G. Farben which were headquartered there, and ensuring that the Rothschild's banking operations in Frankfurt weren't bombed. Frankfurt later became CIA headquarters after the Rothschilds established the Office of Strategic Services to acquire intelligence needed to coordinate troop movements and determine targets to be bombed during the war. Based upon the Venetian spy model, the OSS morphed into the CIA, which didn't protect American interests in so much as it defended the Rothschilds' by serving as the dynasty's personal spy and false flag operation, supplementing the intelligence networks they had built elsewhere, like the Cheka, the Mossad, the SAVAK, and the MI5/ MI6.

World War I claimed the lives of nine million soldiers and wounded 21 million more, with civilian casualties approaching 10 million. The Spanish flu broke out as an epidemic in 1918, claiming the lives of between 20 to 50 million people as the Venetians unleashed chemical warfare on an unsuspecting population to "cleanse" areas of to expand their living space.

In 1922, the Soviet Union and Germany formalized their political and economic relationship in the Treaty of Rapallo, a neutrality pact. As part of this agreement, the German industrialists acquired machinery and weaponry like tanks, airplanes, and toxic chemicals. In return, the Germans were allowed to use Soviet territory for military testing and training, helping the Germans rebuild under the watchful eye of the Rothschilds who controlled both governments. In 1936, the Germans regrouped and marched into the Rhineland to reclaim key industrial areas in violation of the Treaty of Versailles, providing the pretext Rothschild needed for World War II.

The Second World War (1939-1945) was a continuation of the First and designed to completely destroy Germany as a rival to Great Britain while generating the publicity the Rothschilds needed to secure Palestine for the Zionists. The war would also draw the United States into the clutches of hostile foreign interests and provide a pretext the Rothschilds sought to re-establish the Roman Empire on the European continent, restore old Venetian trading routes, and create the infrastructure for a nascent world government, using the European Union as a test case. By claiming that "nationalism" had led to war, the Rothschilds could keep countries tied down and weak to prevent them from gaining sufficient strength or momentum to frustrate Rothschild plans for world domination. At the same time, the United States would be drawn into this web of misery, plunder, and oppression.

The Rothschilds knew just the man who could lead Germany into the Second World War – Adolf Hitler, who was one of their own. An economically and politically unstable Germany gave rise to Hitler and the Nazis, who promptly rearmed and signed strategic alliances with Italy – and Japan, where the Rothschilds and Wall Street were investing in industry.

Before becoming Chancellor of Germany, Hitler was a penniless street cleaner and tramp whose grandfather was Nathan Meyer Rothschild. Maria Schickelgruber, Hitler's grandmother was a maid in the Rothschild's mansion in Vienna in 1836. According to Royal insiders, Maria was subjected to ritual rape by Solomon Mayer Rothschild; Nathan Mayer, Baron de Rothschild; and Lionel Nathan that was designed to inspire the greatest amount of fear and terror in the mother. Once she became pregnant, Maria was sent home to raise the child.

The Rothschilds only marry within their own immediate family to keep the money and power they have accumulated from going elsewhere. As a result, they sired many illegitimate children outside of marriage, often through rape and eugenics programs. Notorious pedophile Jeffrey Epstein, who supplied children for Royal pedophiles and celebrities and who allegedly facilitated adoptions for prominent people, like Supreme Court Justice John Roberts, spoke about "seeding the world" with his sperm, revealing this hidden Rothschild strategy.

The illegitimate children became secret Rothschild agents whose lives were privately supported with Rothschild funding. Hitler's grandmother received child support from a Jewish businessman who served as an intermediary.

Hitler's father was Alois Hitler, an Austrian civil servant in the customs service who had several marriages. Alois Hitler's third marriage was to his own niece, Klara, who became Hitler's mother.

A troubled youth, Hitler wandered the streets and was destitute by the age of 18 when his mother died.

The future Fuehrer lived in a Vienna hostel before he was brought to Britain and trained at the Tavistock Institute in Great Britain for the historic role he would play on the world stage. During his training, he was taught to gesticulate with his hands to emphasize points and trained to mesmerize audiences as a public speaker. He was also indoctrinated in the Big Lie, which the Rothschilds, and their agents have refined to a science, that "nothing is so absurd it will not be believed if it is presented with enough conviction." Hitler followed what he called "the very sound principle" that a big lie is always more credible than a small one. As Queen Elizabeth II's first cousin, Hitler was bred as an agent of war who was given unlimited financial and political support at the right time, Royal insiders said.

Lest there be any doubt about his British training, consider that the Tavistock military psych-op school teaches this principle: "in wartime, the truth is so precious we surround it with a bodyguard of lies." Prime Minister Winston Churchill, a Rothschild bastard and biological father of Queen Elizabeth II, was similarly quoted as saying: "In wartime, the truth is so precious that she would always be attended by a bodyguard of lies." Hitler said: "In wartime we provide truth with a bodyguard of lies because it is so precious." Clearly Hitler was speaking from the British playbook, one written by the Rothschilds.

That Hitler was in England was confirmed by his sister-in-law in her book, *The Memoirs of Bridget Hitler.* Once he settled into his role, Hitler set the stage for Great Britain and France to declare war on Germany to spark World War II. Between 40 and 60 million lives were lost in this war. A product of a secret Rothschild breeding program who was groomed to play an historic role on the world stage, Hitler outlined his grievances in *Mein Kampf* in which he laid out his solution for Germany's ills, that of exterminating the Jewish race.

Hitler was elected Chancellor of Germany in 1933. He then consolidated power, naming himself Fuhrer. He was fixated on the pure German race, to create Lebensraum, or living space, for the German people. While the British imperialists were fixated on the superiority of the Anglo-Saxon race, the Germans were obsessed with their own superiority, perhaps not realizing that the Rothschilds spurred racial superiority among disparate groups as part of a divide-and-conquer strategy. As they move towards their end game of having Communist China rule the world, the Rothschilds indoctrinated the Communist Chinese into believing that their own racial superiority permits them to exterminate Americans and claim North America for themselves to expand their "Lebensraum." Similarly Hispanic activists have been encouraged to reclaim the United States from "evil white Americans" through groups like "La Raza," (which literally means, "the race") to expand their Lebensraum and reclaim it for themselves.

For the most part, these racial identity groups were financed by Big Business and geared at separating people into groups based upon race and grievances. Aggrieved races can then be transformed into conquering armies. Remember that the Rothschild motto is "stronger together." While they conquer the world as a unified force, the targeted populations are separated into groups to weaken them. The Catholic and Protestant churches were even enlisted to the cause through government contracts and community organizers coordinated through the Rothschild-controlled Vatican and World Council of Churches which promoted Marxism behind the banner of religion.

Now, by funding "Black Lives Matter" and ANTIFA, banks and corporations are using grievances to pit races against each other to destroy "white privilege" – that is, any vestige of resistance that stands in the way of Rothschild plans to conquer the United States for Communist China which they control. If white Europeans were rejecting globalism, the dynasty had to identify them as the privileged enemy (the Monarchs of yesteryear) who would need to be sent to reeducation camps, labeled domestic terrorists, and potentially put down so the agenda could continue. The Rothschilds and the Venetians have replayed these tactics over and over again for generations.

After the Nazis took power in 1933, Germany began rearming and militarizing the Rhineland. The British gave them a head start so that Great Britain could be justified in going to war. In 1946, the Rhineland was divided into the newly established states of Hesse, North Rhine-Westphalia, and Rhineland-Palatinate – areas the Rothschilds had dominated for centuries.

While the British were running low on supplies and armaments, they didn't need to scale back their war efforts as the hidden hand had forced President Franklin Delano Roosevelt into signing the Lend-Lease Act to commit the United States into placing the country's wealth and military behind Britain's war effort, whatever the costs. In the process, the British received over $3 billion in war supplies while the American citizens were forced to pay a temporary income tax that became permanent to support the Rothschild agenda for perpetual war and world domination. A once free American people who enjoyed prosperity and abundance were slowly reduced to wage slaves and stripped of their rights. While the Germans tried to negotiate peace with the British, Churchill ignored their pleas understanding that he had unlimited support for war from the U.S. Government.

Nazi leaders made good on their pledge to persecute Jews soon after they assumed power. During the first six years of Hitler's dictatorship, Jews were subjected to more than 400 antisemitic decrees and regulations. For example, the Law for the Restoration of the Professional Civil Service of April 7, 1933, excluded Jews and the "politically unreliable" from civil service. This was followed by the Nuremberg Race Laws which defined Jews not by religious belief but by ancestral lineage. German law also restricted the number of Jewish students at German schools and universities. Other legislation barred Jewish entry into the medical and legal professions. Licenses of Jewish tax consultants were invoked and a quota was placed on the admission of "non-Aryans" to public schools and universities. Jews were even required to register their domestic and foreign property and assets to make it easier for the state to seize their assets.

Once the Second World War commenced, Hitler unleashed

the Final Solution – that of exterminating the Jews, reflecting the death cult of the Venetians. Not only did the Nazis visit Tibet to learn their occult secrets, but the Nazi symbol was based upon it. The vril was identified as a secret source of energy associated with eternal life, the occult, and demonic possession. The Nazis sought to gain knowledge of the vril which was popularized in Britain in Bovril, a popular beef extract used to flavor food.

While Jews were dying in the Holocaust, the Rothschilds ensured that nuclear bombs were dropped on Nagasaki and Hiroshima, decimating flourishing Christian communities in Japan. This was all part of a wider strategy of spreading the "rational Enlightenment" throughout the world by eradicating religion and exterminating those who practiced it.

While the Rothschilds had used opium to subdue the Chinese and hopium to lull Trump supporters into a false sense of security, they used fluoride to dumb down and pacify the public to make them more docile and less likely to respond aggressively to attacks against their country from within and from without.

After the war, the Germans needed to dispose of excess fluoride and so the Mellon Institute recommended adding it to water on grounds that "it may help tooth decay." The shadow elite decided to mix it into water to generate profits for the added benefits – that of increasing infant mortality and rendering people more docile. As they had observed from the concentration camps, fluoride made people more manageable and reduced their capacity to think laterally, that is, it impaired their ability to discern patterns, connect dots, and perceive cause-effect relationships.

After World War II, Baron William Henry Beveridge, a British economist and social reformer, conceived the modern welfare state after Churchill introduced him to socialists Sidney and Beatrice Webb. While the people were told that these programs were designed to help them, the real agenda behind the welfare state was to enhance the competitiveness of British industry by shifting labor costs like healthcare and pensions off corporate ledgers and onto public accounts. Giving money and support to the suffering public would increase their purchasing power so that they could spend more money on products and services sold by these taxpayer-subsidized corporations. Under the Rothschild-envisioned new world order, the world would transform into a welfare state in which the people would be slaves and the corporations would be subsidized by their labor. Power would be consolidated at the top under a tyrannical World Government. As socialist writer H.G. Wells affirmed in *The New World Order* and *The Open Conspiracy:* "This new and complete Revolution we contemplate can be defined in a very few words. It is outright world-socialism; scientifically planned and directed. Countless people will hate the new world order and will die protesting against it. When we attempt to evaluate its promise, we have to bear in mind the distress of a generation or so of malcontents. The term 'internationalism' has been popularized in recent years to cover an interlocking financial, political and economic world force for the purpose of establishing a World Government."

As could be expected, the Rothschilds seized upon the opportunity provided by the two World Wars to plunder. During the first World War, Kaiser Wilhelm II pursued *Kiinstschiitz* to protect precious art work and treasures. As Fuhrer, Hitler seized thousands of paintings and sculptures from Italy, France, Belgium, Russia, Romania, and Poland, all of which were gathered and meticulously inventoried by the Germans. The greed of the Nazis was such that they chipped the gold fillings from the teeth of Jews who had been rounded up and put into concentration camps. According to one report, most of the artwork confiscated by Nazis wound up in Rothschild homes or was donated to museums sponsored by Rothschilds who used museums as public storage units and tax write-offs to maintain overflowing collections of artwork acquired through war, assassinations, revolutions, and outright theft.

The New York Times reported in 2015 that the descendants of Baron and Baroness Alphonse and Clarice de Rothschild donated their collection of 3,500 stolen Nazis treasures to the Museum of Fine Arts in Boston. The collection includes jewelry, jeweled boxes, furniture, prints, drawings, miniatures, tiaras, paintings, and rare books. One Rothschild auctioned off some of the art, collecting

$90 million in the process. Whistle blowers from India have claimed that the gold the Rothschilds stole from Bengal was used to capitalize the Bank of England.

Also revealing the hidden Rothschild hand at work is the curious case of Annc Frank, a Jewish girl whose diary was preserved and published by her father after she died of typhus in the Bergen-Belsen concentration camp. Questioning the circumstances of her diary is not meant in any way to diminish the lives that were lost in this and other concentration camps throughout the World Wars. Nor is it meant to dispute Anne's horrible death at the hands of Nazis.

However, the circumstances surrounding the diary and its publication bear all the marks of Rothschild propaganda campaign to exploit Jewish terror during World War II to promote Zionism. First, Anne's father, Otto Heinrich Frank was a businessman who worked in Frankfurt, Germany, the headquarters of Rothschild banking operations. During World War I, Otto served in the Imperial Army under the Rothschild bastard Kaiser Wilhelm II where he was promoted to lieutenant. It is likely, given this background, that Anne and her family would have received protection from persecution. The camp to which Anne was taken, Bergen-Belsen, was an "exchange camp" and military training camp in which Jewish hostages were exchanged with German prisoners of war held overseas.

Bergen-Belsen just happened to be located in the Province of Hanover, where the Rothschilds had acquired influence and access to the British Royal family. Frank's book describes that while Anne was hiding in Amsterdam from Nazis, she posted pictures of Princess Margaret Rose and her sister, Princess Elizabeth on her walls at a time when the Rothschilds were promoting Elizabeth, a flat lie royal, who was actually Hitler's cousin and a Rothschild bloodline, as a legitimate future Queen. While she was princess, Elizabeth II was given wide publicity for her world tours by the Rothschild-controlled media to enhance her credibility. "I must be seen to be believed," Lilibeth said.

Anne reportedly died in the camp only to have her story

immortalized in an historic museum, with pictures of Elizabeth still hanging on the walls as if part of a carefully crafted narrative.

In 1959, a Swedish journal *Frio Ord* published two articles on the *Diary*, stating: "History has many examples of myths that live a longer and richer life than truth and may become more effective than truth. The Western world has for some years been made aware of a young Jewish girl through the medium of what purports to be her personally written story, *Anne Frank's Diary*. Any informed literary inspection of this book has shown it to have been impossible as the work of a teenager. The New York Supreme Court confirms this point of view, in that the well known American writer, Meyer Levin, has been awarded $50.000 to be paid him by the father of Anne Frank as an honorarium for Levin's work on the *Anne Frank Diary*."

While Anne might have lived and regrettably died in a concentration camp, she didn't write the dairy that bore her name. Moreover, the book became an instant bestseller – which couldn't have happened without support from the Rothschilds who had the ability to prevent the publication of books or promote others to the rank of international bestseller. Not only did Anne's book sell incredibly well, but it was promoted in schools, made required reading for students, and translated into films. The real author, Meyer Levin, was a Zionist who wrote books about Jews traveling to Palestine to escape persecution on behalf of the Rothschilds.

After the World Wars, the Rothschilds convened the Bretton Woods Conference to establish the World Bank and International Monetary Fund, which established global institutional structures to project Venetian mercantilism onto the world stage. Nations set aside precious national assets as collateral for loans whose stringent requirements led to inevitable defaults. Once the country defaulted on the loan, the shadow elite claimed the assets, having invested nothing beyond the public's money. While the Rothschilds grew in wealth, the American middle class was crushed and its standard of living dramatically reduced to subsidize the dynasty's plans for a tyrannical world empire.

After the war, Stalin was allowed a seat on the UN Security

Council, ensuring that the Soviet Union had access to all U.S. troop movements and military strategies. As a result, the United States would never again win another war. Despite having purged Jews from the Soviet Union and Soviet block countries, Stalin supported the UN Partition for Palestine, paving the way for the state of Israel. Three days after Israel declared its independence in 1949, the USSR officially recognized Israel, becoming the second country after the United States to do so. While vehemently antisemitic, Stalin was also pro-Zionist, a pattern consistent among Venetians and their agents. In the quest for world domination, the Rothschilds emerged as the victor, with the headquarters of their global operations established in Israel, a direct affront to all followers of the Abrahamic faiths and to Jews in particular.

Through the World Wars, the Rothschilds laid the foundation for a global government, including a United Nations. After establishing central banks in the countries that were either conquered or were in the process of being conquered by the shadow rulers, the Rothschilds erected the Bank of International Settlements (BIS) as a global central bank.

While originally established to facilitate reparations in Germany after World War I, the BIS morphed into an international institution owned by the 60 (Rothschild-controlled) central banks to "foster international monetary and financial cooperation and (to) serve as a bank for central banks," essentially elevating Rothschild theft to a whole new global level. The Bank was headquartered in Basel, Switzerland where the first Zionist conference was held.

After the Second World War, the Rothschild dynasty endeavored to establish a regional European market on the European continent as part of a plan to resurrect the Roman Empire through the European Coal and Steel Community, which became the European Community, and eventually the European Union. The new regional common market grew to acquire its own currency, army, central bank, and Venetian style republic – including a European Parliament, European Council, and European Commission in which power and wealth were increasingly consolidated into the hands of the few by a government that did not answer or have to be held accountable by the people its leaders claimed to represent. At the same time, the EU engaged in income redistribution schemes to help erect a common market to subsidize, expand, and protect Rothschild business interests while the Rothschilds opened the doors for unrestricted movement within the EU.

Through the European Movement, an organizations launched by Prime Minister Winston Churchill which has branches in London and throughout Europe, the Rothschilds lobbied to have Turkey join the regional market. With the Schengen Agreement in place, allowing Turkey to become an EU member would have allowed its poor Muslim populations visa-free movement throughout the continent and access to Europe's generous entitlement programs. In 1963, plans were laid for Turkey to enter a customs union with the European Union as a step toward EU membership. In 2005, Turkey entered formal discussions to become an EU member.

If it were to become a member, Turkey would be the most populous state, thereby eroding Judeo-Christian values in Europe to accommodate Islam whose adherents sought to impose sharia law and eradicate Judaism and Christianity, with Muslim activists promoting this agenda for the purposes of conquest, reminiscent of the days of the Venetians and their mercenary Turkish forces. Once again, the Rothschilds and their Venetian agents were weaponizing immigration.

Italy in particular is being targeted for destruction as punishment for obstructing Turkey's entry into the EU. Already some classrooms in Italian cities, like Turin, are filled with students, who are not even Italian. Immigrants from African, Syria, and and elsewhere enter Europe through Turkey from states the Rothschild war machine has decimated through war and endless meddling and exploitation. These people have been conditioned to exact their revenge on Europeans and to reject assimilation while forcing European societies to accommodate their cultures, religions and values. Yet, if the Rothschilds cared about protecting Jews, why are they promoting EU membership for Turkey when Muslim immigrants have sought death and destruction of Jews living in Europe, making them feel unsafe in their own countries? This is not meant to be a sweeping generalization of Muslims – but rather to demonstrate that the shadow rulers are weaponizing groups of people to destroy others for the purposes of conquest.

Former French President Nicolas Sarkozy has even spoken out against allowing Turkey to join the European Union, stating, "Turkey has no place in Europe. I have always adhered to this position. It is based on common sense. This does not mean that I have anything against the Turks. We need them. They are our allies in NATO. But if we begin to explain it – that Turkey is in Europe – European school students will have to told that the European border lies in Syria. Where is the common sense? Can Turkey be regarded as a European country culturally, historically, and economically speaking? If we say that, we want the European Union's death."

This is precisely the point. True to Venetian form, the Rothschilds seek to conquer through any means necessary. High atop their agenda is the destruction of Western Civilization, which is based upon Judeo-Christian principles. From the beginning, the Venetians conquerors sought to extinguish the divine right to rule and destroy the true Abrahamic faiths and the followers of these religions.

One website which is promoting the Islamic invasion: (http://aryanism.net/) traces its religious origins not to the Prophet Muhammed but to Asian logic and to Plato, Aristotle, and other philosophers of the rational Enlightenment who seek to eradicate Judeo-Christianity on grounds that these religions have rejected that they believe to be the truth – that is, the Aryan Dharma, which is Buddhist and rejects the values, principles, and teachings of the *Bible*. Even traditional Muslims revere Jesus as a prophet and share many of the same values as their Judeo-Christian counterparts. Not so for the radical Islamists who seek to conquer and destroy Europe and Western Civilization under the banner of Islam. More tellingly, they also champion the Tibetan Buddhists and promote the radical Muslim agenda under the banner of the Nazi symbol.

The elites have opened the doors to foreign invaders from countries the dynasty's war machines have destroyed with a view to seizing the wealth of the Europeans and destroying European values and civilization so that they will never rise up to challenge the Rothschild plan for a new Roman Empire spanning the globe. At the same time, multinationals and international banks are sponsoring racial movements targeting "white supremacy" in which activists burn down cities, attack white people, and demand that whites "surrender their power."

Within the United States, the Federal Reserve was conceived by German banker Paul Warburg, whose relatives are powerful Zionists and German bankers. The Fed was established on Jekyll Island in 1910. In the decades that followed, the American people were robbed of trillions of dollars, with the Rothschilds and their agents rapaciously plundering the public's assets and driving the United States hopelessly into debt.

Originally the U.S. dollar was pegged to the gold standard. Once the Federal Reserve was established, the new central bank was tasked with managing the gold. As with anything entrusted to the Rothschilds, the gold was promptly stolen and traded on the Rothschild's London gold exchange – and then used as a bartering tool to enrich the Rothschilds and their agents further while manipulating markets around the world. Consequently, the United States was taken off the gold standard, allowing the Fed to print unlimited amounts of money to generate wealth for the illegitimate shadow criminal elite all the while reducing the standard of living for everyone else and driving up inflation.

After the dollar was removed from the gold standard, the Rothschilds falsely advised foreign countries, like China and Saudi Arabia, that the dollar was backed by gold and that the federal government could be relied upon to pay its debt. These countries bought U.S. debt which was considered to be a safe investment. In the meantime, the Rothschilds pursued endless spending programs for entitlement programs, corporate bailouts, money for special projects, settlements in the billions of dollars for manufactured grievances, and endless wars for empire, placing the United States in debt to bankers and foreign countries, like China, which the dynasty controls. The Rothschilds then set the stage for Communist Chinese takeover of the United States to fulfill an agenda that was millennia in the making.

The Art of War

Communist China was created by the Rothschilds. In fact, the leader of the Communist Revolution, Chairman Mao Tse-tung, was a product of the secret Rothschild breeding program. Mao's rise to power was coordinated through Yale University, which was founded by Elihu Yale, an English merchant who established Fort St. James for the East India Company. Elihu became the governor of an EIC administration in Madras, India, which was named after Saint James, a Christian Praetorian Guard for Roman Emperor Diocletian, who established the largest and most bureaucratic government in the history of the Roman Empire. Under this empire, taxes were increased to support a sprawling government bureaucracy.

Traditionally, Yale University has recruited the children from families associated with the East India Company or who were otherwise a part of the establishment. A Rothschild-affiliated bank, Brown Brothers Harriman & Co., whose antecedents founded the Second Bank of the United States, established the Yale secret society Skull & Bones, whose members have led intelligence agencies, invested in the corporations that propelled Hitler's war machine, and become Presidents, Senators, and CEOs of multinationals, and media giants.

Working in concert with the Office of Strategic Services (which morphed into the CIA), Yale laid the foundation in China for foreign investment and set the stage for the Chinese Communist Revolution. To this end, Yale divinity school established a branch in China where Mao was tapped, recruited, and indoctrinated in Marxist ideology, preparing him to assume his historic role as leader of the Chinese Cultural Revolution. Mao's army was trained by the OSS. Following in the footsteps of Stalin, Marx, and Engels, Mao became editor of a journal dedicated to "Thought Reorientation." One Yale professor observed that "without Yale, Mao may never have risen from obscurity to command China."

In other words, the United States planted the seeds to its own destruction in Communist China. To support Mao's efforts, Yale paid the rent for Mao's Cultural Book Store, helping the future Communist leader publish *An Introduction to Marx's Capital*, *A Study of the New Russia*, and *The Soviet System in China.* Profits generated from the book sales were invested in a Socialist Youth Crops and the Chinese Communist Party.

Once he was thoroughly indoctrinated, Mao became a delegate to the First Congress of the Chinese Communist Party, which launched the Communist Movement in China. Skull & Bones members worked in China to install Maoists into power, helping them become the largest opium producers, in turn, generating profits for the ruling elite families while preparing the Chinese people for conquest.

Rothschild-controlled media, which was coordinated out of London, promoted Mao's rise with great fanfare. For example, in *Time* magazine, David Rockefeller praised "the real and pervasive dedication of Chairman Mao to Marxist principles," stating that "whatever the price of the Chinese Revolution, it has obviously succeeded in producing more dedicated administration and community of purpose." Rockefeller also affirmed "the enormous social advantages" China acquired through its "singleness of ideology and purpose," which claimed more than 40 million lives. "We, on our part, are faced with the realization that we have largely ignored a country with ¼ of the world's population," Rockefeller said. "The social experiment in China under Chairman Mao's leadership is one of the most important and successful in human history."

Perceiving the threat Mao posed to China, Chiang Kai-shek and his Nationalist Party took over the Chinese government and forced the Yale infiltrators out, only to retreat to Taiwan shortly thereafter. While the U.S. Government paid lip service to Taiwan's nationalism, the actions its political establishment took demonstrate that the loyalties and interests of global elites were aligned with those of the Communist Chinese. To cite but one example, Yale University's newspaper reveled in an American-Chinese communique that announced U.S. troop withdrawal from Taiwan: "Yale scholars seemed pleased and gratified that the United States has chosen to diminish its role in what the experts consistently referred to as a Chinese problem. American troops never belonged in Taiwan to begin with and Taiwan has always been doomed because it refused to surrender its claim to authority over mainland China."

The withdrawal came during the Administration of President Richard Nixon, who normalized U.S.-China relations. Tapped to implement Nixon's China policy was George H.W. Bush, a bonesman who served as Nixon's *de facto* Ambassador to Taiwan before becoming CIA Director and President of the United States. Another notable bonesman, William F. Buckley, the author of *God and Man at Yale* who was credited with launching the modern conservative movement, accompanied Nixon on a trip to China. Secretary of State Henry Kissinger, an ambitious academic affiliated with the Rockefeller-funded Council of Foreign Relations, who served on the Board of Trustees of the Rockefeller Brother's Fund, helped restore relations with China while advancing foreign policy that devastated the United States and the world at large.

Kissinger was mentored by UK Prime Minister Lord Alec Douglas-Home and his associates, including Lord Bertrand Russell, a leading socialist and one world government advocate who trained Mao. After normalizing relations with China, the National Committee of U.S.-China was established in the library of the Church Center of the United Nations building in New York in 1966 with funding from John D. Rockefeller III and the Sloan Foundation, the philanthropic arm of General Motors.

Hillary and Bill Clinton, both Yale graduates, were groomed to advance the agenda further. Reflecting the influence of the hidden hand, Bill Clinton, a poor boy from Arkansas, enjoyed a steep meteoric rise from humble beginnings to become Governor of

Arkansas and then, President of the United States. As the biological son of Winston Churchill and Pamela Harriman, Bill Clinton was the product of the secret Rothschild breeding program who was sent to the United States as a child to fulfill the Atlantic Charter.

As a young man, Clinton was mentored by Arkansas Governor Winthrop Rockefeller who steered his career and connected him to the right people. Reflecting the elite credentials of his biological parents, Harriman married Averell Harriman, a founding Partner of Brown Brothers. Once her son became President, Harriman was appointed Ambassador to France.

Bill Clinton's presidential campaign was bankrolled by Communist China, with both Clintons receiving ample and generous support from the Rothschilds. Upon becoming President, Clinton advanced the globalist agenda through free-trade agreements, like NAFTA, and opened the door for Communist China's entry into the World Trade Organization. Few knew that he was groomed from birth for the historic role he would play on the world stage, though it is widely known that he wasted his year abroad at Oxford University as a Rhodes Scholar smoking pot. However true Rothschild bloodlines don't need to apply themselves. They just need to be malleable puppets. There will always be money available to bail them out, people to run interference for their screw ups, a fawning media to give them favorable press coverage, and endless opportunities for them to earn incredible amounts of money. No wonder, Bill Clinton's unpopular wife, Hillary, expected to be handed the presidency when she thought it was "her turn." The Rothschilds had selected her to preside over the collapse of the United States and its surrender to Communist China. She was all too happy to serve this purpose, with cackling glee.

V.
Resetting the Rothschilds

In recent decades, global elites have transformed China from a sleeping giant into an existential threat to the United States and the world. The conspiracy against humanity has been in play for two millennia, with the Rothschilds seizing upon an ancient Venetian agenda and leading it. There is perhaps nothing more grotesque than the elderly Jacob Rothschild, fourth Baron Rothschild, who in his guttural, affected voice, boasts about the "remarkable" history of his prominent family who somehow managed to become one of the wealthiest dynasties in the world through savvy banking practices, incestuous breeding programs, and good fortune. He waxes on about his gorgeous estates which have amassed tens of thousand works of art, many of which were stolen from fallen aristocrats and Monarchs. His pride in his possessions without a shred of compassion for anyone but himself is truly a sight to behold, like the villain of a Godfather movie.

There is very little to recommend this fiend nor are his stolen collections to be envied. He speaks of how his ancestors arose to fabulous wealth from the "ghettos" of Frankfurt while neglecting to mention the diabolical evil and treachery they committed to arrive at this point. He tries to convince his audience that the Rothschilds' success was due to some innate superiority, cleverness, or good fortune on their part rather than the simple fact that they parasitically attached themselves to others and then weaseled their way into public trust positions, placing leaders and countries into their debt through Babylonian black magic while fomenting Venetian style wars and revolutions to fell nations and governments around the world. Hundreds of millions of people have lost their lives in these wars, and billions have suffered at their hands.

It has been said that a family goes from the castle to the gutter within three generations. It has taken the Rothschilds a few generations longer, given the amount of wealth and power they have accumulated. They never should have been allowed anywhere near power in the first place, nor should anyone have entrusted them with their fortunes, governments, or lives. They were not elected nor do they get to rule humanity unless the people allow them.

In a desperate attempt to salvage the Rothschild legacy, such that it is, Lynn Forester de Rothschild, (Lady de Rothschild) founded the Coalition for Inclusive Capitalism, which she owns with her third husband, Sir Evelyn Robert de Rothschild, an investor with E.L. Rothschild – a firm that manages investments for the Economist Group, which owns the *Economist* magazine; *Congressional Quarterly;* and the *Economist Intelligence Unit.*

If there is any inclusion to be had which involves the Rothschilds, it must move towards a restorative solution in which the dynasty accepts what it has done and makes amends. It's time to restore wealth, power, rights, and self-determination to the people. The Rothschilds and the Venetian agents have created a global mess through their greed, immorality, and arrogance. Since they are the ultimate architects of the global system, the buck stops with them. They must take steps to correct the problems they have created and allow the people to reestablish control over their own countries, release their God-given talents, and nurture their families without the meddling, intrusive hands of the Rothschilds and their agents. By their own standards, their laws are unjust since no one had an opportunity to weigh in on them. No one signed up to be a corporation or a tax slave for a wannabe tyrant.

The Rothschilds have placed their own people into positions of power everywhere creating momentum through institutions, banks, governments, the media, hospitals, armed forces, and other components of society that move in lockstep throughout the world to advance the Venetian agenda. All participants have skin in the game and stand to lose if they abandon it. Yet, humanity loses if they don't.

Everything they have touched, since their agenda has been conceived in "rational self interest" instead of service of God and humanity, has been an unmitigated disaster. Instead of enjoying heaven on earth, they have created hell. They have gained the world and lost their souls. Much of what they destroyed never belonged to them in the first place.

One even wonders if they are capable of considering the human costs of their actions. It's one thing to develop strategies from the ivory tower, to game business and war strategies in board rooms before going off to the cocktail parties while their agents do the dirty work. It isn't just that people's lives are being destroyed – all of life on earth is dying as a direct consequence of their actions. Their green energy projects have killed millions of birds and polluted the grounds. Entire species face extinction. The sustenance people need to survive is being depleted. Entire civilizations and societies have been decimated, mixed up, and compromised all for the ridiculous purpose of amassing money and power for a few undeserving self-appointed elites who seek to use their advantages for wicked, destructive ends that serve no real purpose beyond power for power's sake.

They are so warped in their thinking and steeped in darkness that they see no other way. They have replayed the same agenda over and over generation after generation to arrive at an ending that served to extinguish all of humanity and God's creation. This is a game they cannot win. Even the *Bible* prophesies that the world will descend to unspeakable evil before entering a period of Tribulations and judgment. Then the world will be restored under God's providence. In the game of life, God wins, they lose. All happens in God's perfect timing.

People must go back to putting principle over profits and remember the values that made America the envy of the world, a light unto the darkness, whose people were free and God-fearing. The joy on the faces of Americans from the days gone past has been replaced with fear and cynicism. Humanity must rise up and find its strength and voice, and reject the wicked elites and their miserable agenda.

Remember that actions have consequences. Consider how greatly society benefited and how people rejoiced when God reigned supreme. Think of how far society would have progressed had technology, art, spirituality been directed selflessly in service to mankind rather than selflessly towards greed and power. Centuries of growth and progress in our world have been stifled.

Had the Rothschilds applied their gifts for good, rather than evil, if they sought to serve the people, rather than rob and kill them, imagine where the world would be now. The world we are making today is the one our children and grandchildren will inherit. Careful consideration needs to be given to the values we wish to impart to the world we wish to leave behind.

Society has said "never again" to the Holocaust and yet the perpetrators of this evil have been allowed to perpetuate their agenda against mankind on a global level. They have only been allowed to do this through the complicity of others. The world must recognize who these people are, withdraw their support, and demand accountability. The Rothschilds must correct what they have done, relinquish their power, and then leave the world stage forever, taking their agents with them.

The game was up for the Rothschilds decades ago, and they know this. Russia wrestled free from their system of control as did other countries. Their global financial system was so destructive that other countries began establishing their own financial systems independent of theirs. The illegitimacy and crimes have been exposed and are known to many. Judgment is coming. Instead of inflicting greater harm upon the world for refusing to be destroyed at their hands, they should display some humility and self-awareness, acknowledge their errors with a magnanimous spirit, and take corrective action. Instead they have sought to exterminate humanity and run off with all the loot.

Sadly, the damage they have done to society is so extensive – and yet they keep inflicting more, as if to punish humanity for telling them no! They need to stop and be part of the solution and then step down, recognizing that they are not equipped to rule. God must be restored to the head of society, beginning with the restoration of the divine right.

The Rothschilds don't own the world except through illusion. They have stolen what they have and generated profits based upon nothing that have allowed them to buy everything. Since they think they own it all, they are treating humanity as intruders on their property. Yet they are the bums who have broken into humanity's house and convinced themselves that they now own it.

While they believe humanity must be wiped out to expand their living space, they should recognize that man can now travel to the stars. Scarcity only exists in their minds. Human potential is unlimited and God's bounty is abundant.

In the interests of sustainable development, they seek to deindustrialize the world after rapaciously developing it in pursuit of profits without any consideration to the cost to human life or the environment. Consumerism was brought on by their own materialism. They controlled the companies and media that promoted it. Having acquired the world's wealth, they wish to consolidate their position and force everyone else to downsize while allowing struggling banks to dip into private checking accounts to cover their losses. Their promises are empty, their strategies destructive, and their words are hollow. It's time for them to go.

After the coronavirus destroyed the global economy, Klaus Schwab emerged to lead the way forward through the Great Reset. Yet, he was not elected. Rather, he founded the World Economic Forum as a platform from which to promote his agenda of "fairer outcomes." The people don't need him to decide outcomes. Human potential should be unleashed to allow people to pursue the outcomes of their choice, within an appropriate moral and legal framework. Before he "invented" the Great Reset, Schwab served on the United Nations High Level Advisory Board on Sustainable Development and the UN Committee for Development Planning. He's a Rothschild-created global planner and may for all any of us know be a product of yet another Rothschild breeding program.

Adding to his dubious credentials, Schwab was recognized as a Knight of the *Légion d'Honneur* of France, the highest French order of merit that was established by Rothschild puppet and dictator Napoleon Bonaparte who toppled Monarchs across Europe and promoted "representative governments" at a cost of between five to seven million lives. Schwab was also knighted by Queen Elizabeth II, an illegitimate Monarch and Rothschild bloodline, and awarded the title of Knight Commander of the Order of St. Michael and St. George in recognition of "warrior Christians" who worked with the Knights Templar to plunder for the shadow Venetian elite.

The Sabbatean Frankists

Historians have identified the Rothschilds as members of the Sabbatean cult, which traces to a crazy 17th century character by the name of Sabbatai Levy who believed himself to be the Messiah, not unlike many other Venetian mercenaries who had made similar claims over the centuries. This time it was different, however, since the year was 1666 – with the last three digits representing the number of the beast.

Both Rabbinical Jews and Christians considered Sabbatai Levy to be a heretic. Reflecting his Venetian influences, Levy had deep ties from the Ottoman Empire, where the Sabbateans referred to themselves as Ba'ale Milamah, or warriors. Their members sponsored the Young Turks movement and felled the Ottoman Empire. They were revolutionaries of the Venetian mold. During his lifetime, Messianic fever was at an all time high as London, England was under attack from subversive force that made locals believe they were living through the End Times. Between 1665 and 1666, the Bubonic plague killed about 100,000 people or a quarter of the population of London. In the middle of all this madness, Levy offended a Turkish sultan and then converted to Islam, committing apostasy.

In 1666, the Venetians attempted to seize the British Crown for a powerful warrior-king they would attempt to portray as the Messiah but who was later rejected as the Antichrist. As P*roverbs 16:12* affirmed, the divine rite to rule held that "it is an abomination for Kings to do evil, for the throne is established by righteousness." While the Christian rulers aspired to honesty, the Venetians practiced deceit, treachery, and deception, understanding that "if a ruler listens to a falsehood, all his officials will be wicked." (*Proverbs 29:12*) This suited the shadow elite just fine. If the Venetians were to have a chance at establishing a one world tyrannical government, the *Old Testament* and *New Testament* would need to be eviscerated.

Days before Levy's conversion, a fire blazed through London, destroying 13,200 homes, 87 parish churches, St. Paul's cathedral, and the homes of 70,000 of the City's 80,000 inhabitants. While the public was told they were entering the Rapture, the Venetians were attempting to seize the British Crown through Oliver Cromwell whom some heralded as the Messiah (warrior king) before rejecting him as the Antichrist. Cromwell attempted to consolidate his control over the British people and impose Noahide Laws before he was toppled. Under Cromwell's leadership, English ships established a permanent presence in the Mediterranean, so that they could tap Venetian trade routes.

During the Civil War, Cromwell led the armies of Parliament against the Monarch, resulting in the assassination of King Charles I, the first English King ever to be assassinated. Cromwell's major-general, Thomas Harrison, who had committed the regicide, was then hailed as the Messiah. (Another one!) The conspirators fled to New Haven, Connecticut where they founded Yale University in 1701. After executing the King, Cromwell then established the British Commonwealth and declared himself the rightful heir to the throne. Charles II was restored to power in 1660, reaffirming the divine rite of kings.

By the 18th century, as Rothschild-inspired revolutions were getting underway, Sabbatean Frankism emerged as a religious movement centered on the leadership of yet another Jewish Messiah claimaint Jacob Frank, not to be confused with the numerous other Muslim and Christian claimants.

While Frank professed to be Jewish, rabbis excommunicated him from Judaism for attempting to deify himself through "purification through transgression." He disregarded modesty and morality while promoting licentiousness and degeneracy. Jews, Catholics, Protestans, and Muslims have all tried to convert these people, hoping that by forcing them to adopt a religion and accept a standard of conventional morality, their destructive behavior will stop. While Sabbateans regularly assumed conventional religious identities, they held onto their heretical beliefs which had served them so well. That they were going to hell in a handbasket didn't seem to bother them.

In keeping with their traditions, Napoleon Bonaparte was once considered to be the Messiah as was Adolf Hitler, who sought to destroy all religion to lead the world into a final victory against God's people.

The Rothshild agenda is just the Venetian agenda on steroids. Consider that Communist China unveiled a multi-trillion dollar One Belt One Road project retracing the ancient Venetian trade routes. Rio Tinto, an Anglo-Australian multinational headquartered in London and one the world's second largest metals and mining corporations, has partnered with the nation's federally recognized Indian Tribes, like the Cheyenne River Soul Tribe, and Army Corps of Engineers on mining projects, with the Rothschilds controlling both the tribes and the military. Rio Tinto purchased British Petroleum's failing mining unit for $4.3 billion in 1989 and recently partnered with Mongolia in South Gobi to tap one of the largest known copper and gold deposits in the world. The Oyu Tologi mining pit is the largest industrial complex ever built in Mongolia and is owned jointly by the government of Mongolia and Rio Tinto, a Rothschild-controlled company. Few are aware of the power and wealth the Mongolians have nor how they managed to acquire it.

The Venetian influence was also apparent in the controversies surrounding the 2020 presidential election, with Maria Zack from Nations in Action alleging vote tampering involving embassy officials in Rome and the Vatican. And then there was the reported firefight at CIA headquarters in Frankfurt. Anticipating foreign interference in the election, Trump signed an Executive Order in 2018 that would have preserved the integrity of the nation's elections in 2020 – and yet he was prevented from enacting these orders by forces unseen. Israeli Prime Minister Bibi

Netanyahu was among the first to congratulate Biden on his victory even while the election results were still in dispute.

The nation's media and politicians then lined up behind Biden, perhaps in fear of the hidden hand, which was frustrated with Trump's refusal to accommodate demands for strikes against Syria and Iran and the green energy agenda which seeks to deindustrialize the United States and impose a technocracy on the American people, reflecting the influence the shadow Venetians. Even Trump seemed disinterested in challenging the election fraud despite evidence provided by attorneys like Sidney Powell, and My Pillow CEO Mike Lindell. It was as if Trump's hands were tied. Once Biden was inaugurated, the globalist foreign policy agenda was back on track. Somehow this time, the wind had been removed from their sails, slackening the pace of the imperialists.

Problems with Q-Anon

On January 6, 2021, patriots and Q-Anon supporters convened on Capitol Hill demanding that the Electoral College authenticate the results of the presidential election based upon the popular vote. At the same time, Trump's own attorney, Rudy Giuliani, demanded "trial by combat." Among the protesters to storm the Capitol was not an Israeli or cross-bearing Christian, but a "Q-Anon supporter" dressed as a shaman. Incredibly, video appears to show security opening the doors to Congressional chambers to let him in, providing the pretext the shadow hand needed to crack down on patriots by making them out to be violent revolutionaries who were trying to overturn an election.

Q-Anon is widely accepted as a psych-op designed to mislead the public by mixing truth with fantasy to manipulate the emotions of vulnerable patriots who feel powerless in the face of pervasive corruption within their government. Since the January 6 offensive, patriots have been censored, deplatformed, and defunded, reflecting a Venetian-style crackdown. The attacks against patriots are reminiscent of the Nuremberg Laws that targeted Jews in Nazi

Germany.

Q-Anon, which references the highest level (Q) security clearance that the Queen of England holds over the British colony of the United States, identifies with the Byzantine Empire, as Professor of Art History Roland Betancourt from UC Irvine discovered: "From Charlottesville to the Capitol, medieval imagery has been repeatedly shown at far right rallies and riots. Displays of Crusader shields and tattoos derived from Norse and Celtic symbols are of little surprise to medieval historians like me who have long documented the appropriation of the Middle Ages by the far right."

Q-Anon activists have been shown wearing red crosses, scapegoating Jews, and dressing as the Knights Templar while promoting the restoration of the old Byzantine Empire. Betancourt documented the Byzantine symbolism used by far-right "neo-Nazis" in a "Unite the Right" rally in Charlottesville, Virginia. Among the movement's supporters is a new supremacist group emerged called "The New Byzantium project." (www.byzantiumnovum.org). Its members "are considered to hold dual-citizenship along with the citizenship of the nations in which they currently hold legal status," just as the Venetians have always done.

The New Byzantine's premise is that "when Rome fell, the Byzantine Empire went on to preserve a white-European civilization," Betancourt said, only "this isn't true. In reality, the empire was made up of diverse peoples who walked the streets of its capital, coming from as far away as Nubia, Ethiopia, Syria and North Africa."

The Byzantines established trade routes throughout these and other areas with the Venetians and their mercenary forces to enslave people, conquer lands, and peddle their goods. Their mercenaries were known for their deception, one of professing one agenda while pursuing another. While the "new Byzantine" project has announced plans to "preserve white dominance," its activities have achieved the opposite, allowing radicals to make claims about dangerous "white supremacists" that do not reflect either the mindset or behavior of most white American patriots. Instead, these claims have justified silencing anyone who can be tarred with this label.

At the same time, decent white Christians, who don't have an ounce of racism in their bodies and whose ancestors were not slave owners, have been persecuted by agents of a shadow hand that has striven for centuries to conquer Judeo-Christian Europe.

While Q-Anon has told its followers to "trust the plan" as one would God, the movement is rife with Byzantine references and hopium: "Through my research, I have monitored references of Byzantium in online forums," Bentacourt wrote. "Mentions of Byzantium are scattered across message boards frequented by both white supremacists and Q-Anon enthusiasts – who spout conspiracy theories about a Deep State cabal of Satan-worshiping, blood-drinking pedophiles running the world. Across 8kun and other online platforms I have reviewed, the Byzantine Empire is discussed as either continuing the legacy of Rome after it was, in their understanding, destroyed by the Jews or being the only true empire, with Rome being merely a historical myth created to degrade Byzantium's power and importance."

Antisemitism was inspired by the Venetians and their mercenary forces who pretended to be Jews (just as they pretended to be Christians and Muslims) in order to claim the Jewish identity and destiny. They have scapegoated Jews throughout history. "Q-Anon commentators across message boards and Twitter speak of the "exiled throne of Byzantium," Bentacourt wrote. "The Empire never went away, it just went occult." These same posters demand a "return to Byzantium" to "save the people from Satanists," while smearing the real Christians and Jews through association with a movement associated with violent white supremacists and thugs at a time when real patriots are actually law abiding citizens are exposing the pedophile rings – the glue that holds a shadow cabal together worldwide, as revealed through the Jeffrey Epstein and Jimmy Savile scandals.

The Q-Anon promoters clearly understand that Jews and Christians would naturally be horrified and repulsed by pedophilia and the dark occult practices of the shamans. Appreciating the patriots' deep affection for President John F. Kennedy, who courageously challenged the Deep State, one Q-Anon commentator claimed to be the real JFK, Jr., the son of the President who died in a helicopter crash before a New York Senate run, clearing the path for Hillary Clinton to become Senator.

In other words, the hidden hand is mixing truth – exposure of pedophile rings to corral true people of God into one camp – with fiction to lead them on a path to their own destruction. This tactic is a script taken right out of the Mongolian playbook. If the Q-Anon movement were real, why are the highly publicized Q activists dressing as shamans and Knights Templar rather than normal, respectable Christian and Jewish patriots? Q-Anon underscored the importance of symbolism, affirming that "symbolism will be their downfall."

Bentacourt has characterized Trump's affinity with Russian President Vladimir Putin as somehow tied into the Q-Anon movement based upon Russia's aspirations to built the "Third Rome." However, the Third Rome is a centuries-old goal established by Byzantine Christians who fled the old Empire to escape violent persecution by Byzantine heretics. The persecuted sought to preserve Christianity and Judaism and establish God's kingdom centered around the Third Rome. Real Christians and Jews aren't white supremacists or Nazis nor do they engage in "trial by combat." These are all tactics of the hidden hand.

The Sun and the Moonies

The Anglo-Zionist agenda that currently afflicts America is a Venetian cancer. Consider the curious case of Rev. Sun Myung Moon, whose cult personifies the Venetian spiritual merchant-warrior class, but for conservatives. As the *Executive Intelligence Report* reported in 2002, Rev. Moon is the "titular head of a multi-trillion-dollar, worldwide apparatus of government influence-peddling and control that knows no equal." The Moonie cult leader "literally owns whole countries in South America and Asia (and his) apparatus is rapidly buying up the U.S. Congress, the Presidency, and all potential opposition forces of left, right, and center. Rev. Moon's stock-in-trade is cash and sex, lots of it. The cash comes from the worldwide drug- and gun-running operations, part of which came to the surface in the Iran-Contra scandal: cocaine from the South American trade run."

The Unification Church over which Rev. Moon presides, works hand-in-hand with the Zionists and has emulated the Venetian/Zionist blackmail/influence peddling rings. In the 1970s and 1980, Rev. Moon's Unification Church was involved in sex trafficking. As the *EIR* reported, conservative political and military officials were enticed to join the movement by participating in weekly orgies, arranged by Col. Bo Hi Pak, the Unification Church officer who worked for the Korean Central Intelligence Agency (KCIA). The KCIA was created by the CIA, which was based upon the OSS/MI5/MI6 and which is enjoined with a Venetian/Mossad intelligence gathering network to protect and advance the interests of the shadow elite.

The Moonies are said to "own the religious right" and are heavily invested in the business of the Nation of Islam's Louis Farrakhan, who blames Jews for the world's ills in true Venetian fashion. Among Rev. Moon's assets are reportedly the Rev. Jerry Falwell, a prominent Christian Zionist. The Reverend has also "bought up most of the independent black churches, (and) uses his ample supplies of money, gold-plated watches minted in his own factories, and his private stock of Asian brides for the most corrupt."

After September 11, 2001, Rev. Moon made significant inroads into traditional religious Muslim communities and mosques around America which were then speaking about establishing a caliphate over America – that is, imposing strict sharia law over the United States and conquering the country by out-breeding Americans to bring in waves of fertile women and military age men antagonistic to the United States who could produce lots of children, stage terrorist attacks, and live on the dole while forcing American taxpayers to subsidize them and surrender their civil liberties. At the same time, speaking out against these policies was characterized as "Islamophobic" while Americans were depleted of their assets and stripped of their freedoms, making them less likely to have children, as they simply couldn't afford to raise them and didn't want to bring children into a hostile world. The Venetians were once again attempting to conquer the United States and destroy Judeo-Christian culture, religions, and peoples, with the help of treasonous politicians.

The wealth of Venetian mercenaries is staggering. By some accounts, some Rothschilds and Mongolian Khans were trillionaires. Trillions have reportedly been shored up at the Vatican, and then there are the vast vaults filled with gold. Given the control they have wielded, it is not surprising that Venetian agents have come out of nowhere to head multi-billion dollar tech companies launched in garages that have deep ties with the military-industrial complex and which are constructing a vast Venetian-style surveillance grid around our lives.

Once America's corrupt politicians succumbed to bribery and influence, they kowtowed to foreign interests, typically reaching their hands into the deepest of pockets since they relied so heavily upon campaign contributions. Through the International Conferences for the Unity of Science and Federation of World Professors, Rev. Moon paid six-digit honoraria to leading scientists, so that they would use their reputations to promote population control, artificial intelligence, and world federalism," all goals that coincide with the globalist agenda.

Population control is very important to elites who seek "Lebensraum," or living space through population reduction by way of abortions, wars, chemical warfare, and pandemics. Through artificial intelligence, they can reduce their need for people and erect an oppressive surveillance control grid. World federalism promotes an emerging global government under the United Nations. The Moonies underwrite the conservative *Washington Times* and *United Press International,* and Rev. Moon "controls industries around the world, ranging from food production and distribution to arms manufacturers, including the original producers of the Thompson sub-machine gun."

The crossover between the Moonies, radical Islam, establishment globalists, and Anglo-Zionists is uncanny: Zionist "Sen. Joseph Lieberman (D-Conn.) received the 2002 Truman-Reagan Freedom Award from the Moonie front group, the Victims of Communism Memorial Foundation," the *EIR* reported. "In 2000, (Zionist) Sen. John McCain (R-Ariz.) presided over the award presentation. The President of this Foundation, Lee Edwards, is the Editor of the Sun Myung Moon magazine, *The World and I.* Its Public Liaison Officer is Society Editor of Moon's *Washington Times.* Included on the National Advisory Council of this Moonie front are: former National Security Adviser Zbigniew Brzezinski; former Senators Robert Dole, Dennis DeConcini, and Claiborne Pell; former UN Ambassador and now head of the American Enterprise Institute Jeane Kirkpatrick; the head of the Heritage Foundation; and many more officials of respectable organizations and talking heads you see on television every day."

The political elite beat a path to Rev. Moon's door. On February 27, 2021, the Moonies held a global Rally of Hope conference (https://rallyofhope.us/) entitled "From Pandemic to Peace" which was organized by the Universal Peace Federation, a group holding General Consultative Status with the Economic and Social Council of the United Nations. Among the keynote speakers were Pastor Paula White, Trump's spiritual advisor; United Nations World Food Program Executive Director David Beasley; India Vice President Mohammad Hamid Ansari; H.E. Jose Manuel Barroso, former President of the European Commission; Vice President Mike Pence, South Africa President F.W. de Klerk; and such high profile Zionists as former Newt Gingrich and former Vice President Dick Cheney.

While Moon affirms that he will "devote the remainder of my life to ending war, immorality, and greed, and liberating God's heart so that we can build a world overflowing with true peace and love," his keynote speakers promote endless war, live morally compromised lives, advocate socialist income redistribution schemes, and would say/do anything for profits and promotion, based upon their track records.

Sarah Gilbert, a professor of vaccinology in the Nuffield Department of Medicine at the University of Oxford, was another featured guest at the Moonie conference, keeping in line with the plans laid out by the World Health Organization (WHO), which is bankrolled by leading global technocrat Bill Gates. While working on the AstraZeneca COVID-19 vaccine, Gilbert said that she and her team share the idea of caring for fellow beings. "The values that resulted in this vaccine being made available align with those of the Universal Peace Federation," she said. "This vaccine was made for all of us, to protect each other and ourselves. We still have more to do, but the work of our international team has paid off, and the vaccine we made is already saving lives."

To understand where the globalists want to take us, Tedros Adhanom, the WHO Secretary General, has advocated eliminating currency in the interests of public health. With an insufficient social credit score, a person can be prevented from participating in society through travel passports which require vaccinations; deplatformed for politically incorrect speech, and demonetized for expressing the wrong opinion. In this way, shadow elites can determine how much wealth people are allowed to make and spend and under what circumstances.

In his address to the Moonies, Pence, who professes to be an Evangelical Christian, said that he will work with other countries to challenge China's rise as an economic and military power. "We will stand firm against our common adversaries even as we work in good faith to turn our adversaries into friends," he said.

Making China a friend should be an easy feat considering that Wall Street and the Venetian networks established Communist China in the first place. The template China established for a global control system – though social credit scores and track and trace technology -- is now being applied in the United States and elsewhere. The purpose of the conference, Rev. Moon said, is to "build partnerships for peace based upon interdependence, mutual prosperity, and universal values," reflecting a world in which virtue-signaling shadow elites dictate values; globalism takes precedence over national sovereignty; "universal values" override religious, personal, and national preferences; and elites enrich each other while pursuing "sustainable development" for the farm animals.

As the Moonies affirm in a press release: "It is important to commit to international cooperation and multilateralism. Climate change, trade issues, and global pandemics all require an international response. The vocabulary we use to talk about these issues -- calling them threats that have the potential to cause extinction – is unnecessarily pessimistic. It is necessary to convince the world that these problems can be solved and that cooperation can be productive and reliable. We must convince the world that hope is stronger than fear." Judaism, Christianity, and Islam have been co-opted to advance globalism.

Not unsurprisingly, Rev. Moon was recruited and trained by British intelligence operations, including, the socialist Bertrand Russell and H.G. Wells, who authored *Open Conspiracy: Blue Prints for a World Revolution.* Wells identifies religion as a tool for power and social control, giving rise to Rev. Moon's Gnostic sex cult which advocates the end of nations. To achieve this, the *EIR* reported, the Moonies have sought to eliminate all philosophical, cultural, and religious traditions. Its One World Religion seeks to eliminate once and for all the divine right to rule, setting the stage for shadow elites to rule as Gods on earth. This is one arm of the Hegelian dialectic which seeks to advance conservatism as an antidote to the Antichrist of communism by moving society forward towards a more (rational) Enlightened future to secure the rule of the few over the many. Among the supporters of Rev. Moon are Tibetan Buddhist's Dalai Lama – who has attended Moonie meetings alongside Jewish, Islamic, and Christian leaders who view Italian dictator Benito Mussolini as the "perfect fascist."

Bertrand Russell was the grandson of Lord John Russell, who was Prime Minister during the reign of Queen Victoria when the Rothschilds were in full control of the British Parliament and Monarchy. The senior Russell worked alongside the British spymaster and head of the Foreign Office, Lord Palmerston, who groomed such revolutionaries as Giuseppe Mazzini and Karl Marx.

The Venetians are obsessed with controlling Jerusalem.

Reflecting the shamanistic principles of the Venetian mercenaries, Moon was described by the *EIR* as having "converted to a Pentecostal sect of the Presbyterian Church. Under North Korean Communist rule in 1946, Moon set up his own Pentecostal church, called the Jerusalem of the East (Kwang-ya) (featuring) shouting, faith-healing, and a Moon innovation called blood-sharing. Based on pagan fertility rites, this was unlimited copulation of the pastor with his female followers." The Moonies were fighting Communism while backed by interests promoting Communism. They are the insurgents who are fighting the counterinsurgents while both are leading humanity to the same hell-bound destination.

Consistent with the principles of the rational Enlightenment, the Moonies believe that people can be programmed like computers. To this end, they seek to dumb people down to render them less resistant to a new world order. "The unifying theme was the denial of the nobility of man, as expressed in the provable power of the human mind to create and discover new ideas," the *EIR* reported. "For the no-soul gang, there is no distinction of man from the beast, nor even from inorganic matter. There is, thus, no soul. To maintain such a view, creative reason must be denied. The mind must be shown to be merely a formal-logical processor, no different from a digital computer. The method of knowing the world is reduced to analysis of sensory data received at the nerve endings."

According to scientific reports, the elites have mapped out the genome to determine the precise gene through which a person's soul connects with the Creator and have sought too eliminate or deaden that aspect of the person to make him more controllable. They seek to transform people into automatons who simply follows orders absent God or conscience.

The Moonie vision for the future mirrors that of the Venetians – one in which effete, degenerate elites happily preside over the oppressed, dumbed down masses while going about their vacuous day, one filled with pleasures, sensual indulgence, without a care in the world while the brute slaves toil for them. Key to achieving this agenda is eliminating critical thinking and serious study of the sciences and the arts to manipulate people by emotion.

This strategy appears to have taken a life of its own in the Q-Anon movement in which desperate patriots were manipulated through emotions to suspend critical thinking to accept that they would awaken from the nightmare that was descending upon their country and move effortlessly into an Utopian future in which everything magically transformed while the public did nothing beyond "trust the plan."

"Moon's is a Gnostic doctrine, not of his own invention," the *EIR* reported. "The method of propagating cults as a means of maintaining subject populations under the rule of an imperial power, goes back at least as far in known history as the Babylonian Empire. The Romans learned it from the high priests of the East, whence it passed along, by way of Byzantium, to Venice, the leading maritime power up to the 17th Century. From Venice, it penetrated into England, and eventually became a standard piece in the repertory of the British Empire's intelligence services. The specific cult doctrine known as Gnosticism came to the Hellenic world by way of the Persian domination of Mesopotamia. It originated as a form of mystery worship of astronomical deities. The number seven has mystical significance as the number of the five visible planets, plus the Sun and Moon."

The Moonies aligned with one of the most fascist parties in Japan and and even lobbied to have Japan bomb Pearl Harbor to draw the United States into the Second World War. Rev. Moon reportedly trafficked in heroin and helped launch U.S. television ministries that preach the prosperity gospel while sitting on $1 billion in savings. The prosperity gospel promoted by the nation's mega-churches were born out of the technocratic movement.

The Moonies even own a gun company called Kah Arms in which they profess to be "locked and loaded for the Lord." While advocating peace, they have reportedly sold guns to Israel that were used to kill the Palestinians. They are even caught trying to usher in the End Times by attempting to stage nuclear holocausts and other End Times scenarios for this purpose. Some Moonies have even photographed themselves wearing a crown of bullets. They are the ultimate heretics who have proclaimed themselves the Messiah in the style of the Venetians.

Should there be any doubt about the shadow Venetian agenda in play, consider that the three most powerful cities in the world are London, which controls international finance; Washington, DC, which harbors the world's military; and the Vatican, which both holds the Rothschild's wealth and acts as the world's moral authority. Each of these cities is graced with "Cleopatra's Needle" – that is, a symbolic phallus in the shape of an obelisk that is surrounded by a circle, representing the female genitalia – or the sexual union of Julius Caesar and Cleopatra, which produced a would-be heir to the Roman Empire. This is a tribute to ancient Gods whom the shadow elite worship with a view to rebuilding the Roman Empire with themselves as hereditary dictators. Once God's people awaken to the agenda and the traitors lurking in the shadows, they can take measures to rout out the cancer, heal the world, and restore God's rightful place in society.